M. Long...

KU-476-741

M. Long...

Dinosaurs written by: Anthony Harvey
Illustrated by: Alan Male, Lawrence Mynot, Colin Newman,
                David Pickard, Geoff Taylor.

Creatures written by: Michael Gabb
Illustrated by: Alan Baker, Oriol Bath, Chris King, Alan Male,
                Patricia Mynot, Nina Roberts, Pru. Theobalds,
                Steve Thomas, Mike Woodhatch.

Designed by: Tri-Art
Series Editor: Christopher Tunney
Art Director: Keith Groom

©Christensen Press Limited 1984

Originally published as separate titles in 1978 by Sackett
and Marshall Limited. This edition published 1984 by Christensen
Press Limited.

All rights reserved. No part of this publication may be reproduced,
stored in a retrieval system, or transmitted in any form or by
any means, electronic, mechanical, photocopying, recording, or
otherwise, without the prior written permission of the Publisher.

Printed and bound by Graficas Reunidas, Madrid, Spain.

ISBN: 0 946994 03 X

Dinosaurs

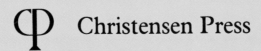

Christensen Press

How do we know about the past?

EXPLORING THE PAST For hundreds of millions of years before human beings existed, the Earth was populated by many different kinds of animals that have since become extinct —that is, animals that have died out. Among them were the reptiles called dinosaurs.

Our knowledge of prehistoric life comes from fossils—remains or impressions of animals and plants that have been preserved in the rocks for millions of years. Skeletons and parts of skeletons of many prehistoric animals have been found. But few fossils remain of animals without hard parts.

Brontosaurus

When fossilized bones are discovered, they are carefully assembled to re-create a skeleton.

Sometimes, an outline in carbon of an animal's complete body can be seen.

Ichthyosaurus

How have the skeletons of prehistoric animals been preserved?

A sea reptile dies, and sinks to the sea bed.

Its body decays, and its skeleton is covered by layers of mud.

Most fossils are found in sedimentary rocks—rocks formed when sand grains and other particles settled in layers and then hardened.

The mud hardens into rock. The skeleton is slowly petrified.

Earth movements raise the sea bed. The rock wears away to reveal the fossilized skeleton.

What other kinds of fossils are there?

Some fossils are the remains of animals that have been *petrified* (turned to stone). Water seeping through the rock has dissolved away the original substance of the animal, and deposited minerals in its place. An exact copy of the original has been formed. Sometimes, no minerals are deposited, and only an empty mold remains. This still shows the shape of the animal.

Fish skeleton preserved when minerals filled air spaces in bones

Leaf preserved for millions of years

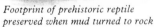

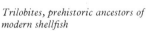

Trilobites, prehistoric ancestors of modern shellfish

Footprint of prehistoric reptile preserved when mud turned to rock

How do we know their age?

Mammoth of Long Ago

Sometimes whole animals have been found preserved in tar swamps or in ice for thousands of years.

The prehistoric animals called Graptolites help in dating rocks because their shape changed at different periods.

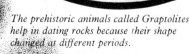

Cenozoic Era

Mesozoic Era

Paleozoic Era

The rocks that make up the Earth's crust lie in layers, one on top of the other. These layers were formed at various periods of the Earth's history. By radio-carbon dating, and in other ways, scientists can tell approximately when each layer was formed. If there are animal fossils in a layer, and the layer has been dated, scientists know how long ago the animal lived. The process works the other way around, too. Fossils help to date rocks.

The Dinosaurs' Place in Prehistoric Life

Medusae

Nautiloids

Meganeura

Worms

Gordonia

Snails

Tanystropheus

Dinichthys

Archaeopteryx

Edaphosaurus

Moschops

Phytosaur

Rhamphorhynchus

Dimetrodon

Saltoposuchus

Scelidosaurus

Henodus

Elasmosaurus

Brachiosaurus

Diplodocus

Stegosaurus

MESOZOIC ERA

CENOZOIC ERA

NEOZOIC ERA

Protoceratops

Pteranodon

Iguanodon

Tyrannosaurus

Palaeoscincus

Triceratops

Tylosaurus

Phenacodus

Barylambda

Opossum

Alticamelus

Hypolagus

Dinotherium

Uintatherium

Protosiren

Diatryma

Baluchitherium

Human

Mammoth

Megatherium

Osteoborus

REPTILES RULE THE WORLD The animal kingdom has two main groups—invertebrates and vertebrates. The invertebrates are animals without a backbone. The vertebrates have a backbone: they are the fishes, amphibians, reptiles, birds, and mammals. The first reptiles appeared on Earth about 300 million years ago, and reached their peak in Mesozoic times. Before them, fishes and amphibians had existed, but the reptiles were the first animals that were able to spend their whole lives on land. The amphibians were able to live on land—as frogs and toads do today—but had to return to water to lay their eggs. Many reptiles still exist today. But many others have become extinct. The flying reptiles and the great sea-monsters—the ichthyosaurs and plesiosaurs—have died out.

What is a reptile?

Reptiles are cold-blooded animals. Unlike mammals and birds, they cannot control the temperature of their bodies. Their movements depend on the temperature of the place in which they live. On a warm day, they are active. On a cold day, they hardly move at all. Nearly all reptiles lay eggs, though in some species the young are born alive. The eggs are laid on land, and the young hatch out as exact miniatures of the adults. The parents show no interest in their young.

Protoceratops

Do modern reptiles have prehistoric ancestors?

The reptiles of today are found in the warmer parts of the world. They live on land, in rivers, and in the sea. The most common reptiles are snakes and lizards. Crocodiles are the only archosaurs left. In fresh water, there are terrapins. And in the sea, there are turtles, some of which are enormous. Tortoises, which live on land, can weigh up to 350 lb (160 kg). These giants are found on oceanic islands, such as the Galápagos in the Pacific Ocean.

Alligator

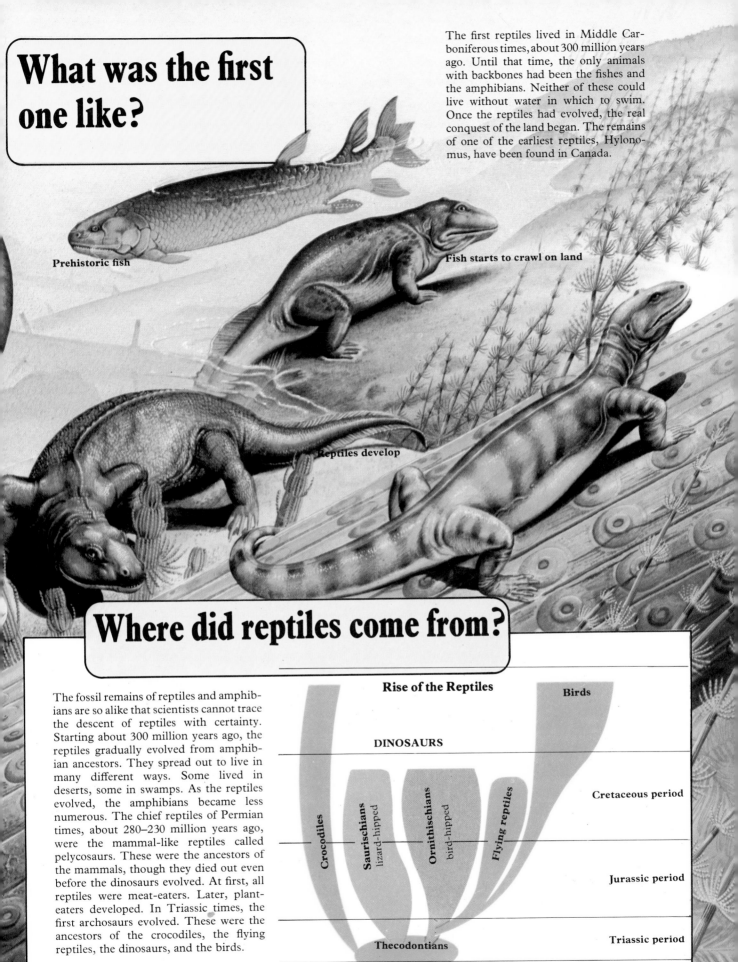

What was the first one like?

The first reptiles lived in Middle Carboniferous times, about 300 million years ago. Until that time, the only animals with backbones had been the fishes and the amphibians. Neither of these could live without water in which to swim. Once the reptiles had evolved, the real conquest of the land began. The remains of one of the earliest reptiles, Hylonomus, have been found in Canada.

Prehistoric fish

Fish starts to crawl on land

Reptiles develop

Where did reptiles come from?

The fossil remains of reptiles and amphibians are so alike that scientists cannot trace the descent of reptiles with certainty. Starting about 300 million years ago, the reptiles gradually evolved from amphibian ancestors. They spread out to live in many different ways. Some lived in deserts, some in swamps. As the reptiles evolved, the amphibians became less numerous. The chief reptiles of Permian times, about 280–230 million years ago, were the mammal-like reptiles called pelycosaurs. These were the ancestors of the mammals, though they died out even before the dinosaurs evolved. At first, all reptiles were meat-eaters. Later, plant-eaters developed. In Triassic times, the first archosaurs evolved. These were the ancestors of the crocodiles, the flying reptiles, the dinosaurs, and the birds.

Rise of the Reptiles

Birds

DINOSAURS

Crocodiles

Saurischians
lizard-hipped

Ornithischians
bird-hipped

Flying reptiles

Cretaceous period

Jurassic period

Thecodontians

Triassic period

How big were the dinosaurs?

THE AGE OF DINOSAURS Dinosaurs—th[e] name means "terrible lizards"—were the co[m]monest animals on Earth for nearly 150 milli[on] years. They first appeared about 200 milli[on] years ago. Many of them were not terrible at a[ll.] Some were big, slow, lazy creatures, and othe[rs] were spritely little animals. But one dinosa[ur,] Tyrannosaurus, was probably the most ter[ri-]fying and savage land animal that ever existe[d.] The dinosaurs had many different ways of li[fe] and made their homes in all kinds of plac[es.] Some of them lived in swampy lowlands, so[me] in wooded regions, and some in semi-dese[rt] uplands.

Some of the big dinosaurs were as tall as a three-story building. They seemed to have little in common with other dinosaurs who were only the size of hens. But they had all evolved from the same ancestors. Meat-eating dinosaurs had sharp teeth and long, strong claws. The plant-eaters often had armor or horns with which to protect themselves. One group, the ankylosaurs, were like walking tanks. They were covered with heavy, bony plates—a kind of armor-plating.

Pteranodon

Brachiosaurus

Allosaurus

321

Were there many different kinds?

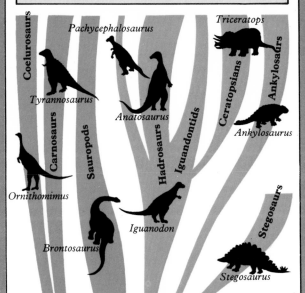

Coelurosaurs
Pachycephalosaurus
Triceratops
Tyrannosaurus
Ceratopsians
Ankylosaurs
Carnosaurs
Anatosaurus
Ankylosaurus
Sauropods
Hadrosaurs
Iguanodontids
Ornithomimus
Iguanodon
Stegosaurs
Brontosaurus
Stegosaurus

SAURISCHIANS ORNITHISCHIANS

Dinosaurs were divided into two main types, called *saurischians* and *ornithischians*. The saurischians included sauropods and theropods. Examples of sauropods were the large plant-eaters *Diplodocus* and *Brachiosaurus*. The theropods were flesh-eaters, and were strong and ferocious. *Tyrannosaurus* was a theropod. The ornithischians were all plant-eaters. There were four major groups of them.

Dinosaur Decoration

Polish stamp with picture of the pelycosaur Dimetrodon

In the world of 200 million years ago, the dinosaurs were very ordinary animals. But to us, they are strange and almost unreal—like creatures from another planet. Because we are fascinated by them, we use pictures of them to decorate all kinds of objects, from table-mats to stamps.

What was the first dinosaur?

It is not certain which was the first real dinosaur, but one of the first was *Ornithosuchus*, a creature about 6 feet (2 meters) long. It was an ancestor of the great *Tyrannosaurus*. Like *Tyrannosaurus*, it was a flesh-eater, as were all the first dinosaurs. It preyed on plant-eating reptiles. The first plant-eating dinosaur appeared at the very end of the Triassic period.

How long did the age of dinosaurs last?

Dinosaurs

Humans

The first of the dinosaurs lived about 200 million years ago. They evolved into a great variety of animals, and adapted themselves to widely differing environments. During Jurassic and Cretaceous times, they dominated all other land animals. They lived for about 150 million years before becoming extinct. Human beings have lived for only about 40,000 years.

What color were dinosaurs?

Nobody knows for certain what color dinosaurs were. But it is probable that, like most reptiles, they had dull brownish or greenish skins. Their coloring would have helped to camouflage them, or to frighten away enemies. Many animals of today have coloring that serves these purposes. Only in a few cases has dinosaur skin been preserved as a fossil. Even when it has been found, the pigment cells have seldom been in existence.

WHAT DINOSAURS WERE LIKE By studying the fossil remains of dinosaurs, it is possible to build up a vivid picture of the way that they lived and the world they lived in. From the rocks in which the fossils have been found—and from other evidence—we know the periods of the world's history during which the dinosaurs were the dominant creatures. The skeletons themselves tell scientists how large or how small each dinosaur was. They also help scientists to discover how the animals moved, and what type of food they ate. Fossils of dinosaurs' eggs provide information about the animals' early life. Some of these fossilized eggs contain unhatched baby dinosaurs. The appearance of dinosaurs can sometimes be discovered by examining fossilized skin impressions. Unfortunately, few of these have been found.

Did they walk on all fours?

In some rock strata, the actual footprints made by dinosaurs as they crossed the sandy shores of a sea or lake have been preserved. People searching for fossils have sometimes been able to uncover long trackways of such footprints. These show how the dinosaurs that made them walked —whether on two legs or on four. From tracks left, scientists have also learned other facts—for example, that some dinosaurs lived in herds. Of course, a dinosaur's skeleton may also reveal how it walked.

What were their eggs like?

As dinosaurs were reptiles, they laid eggs. Occasionally, the eggs have been found as fossils. But such fossils are rare. Because dinosaur eggs were fragile, they seldom survived to become fossilized. About 50 years ago, nests of eggs of the *Protoceratops* were discovered in Mongolia. The eggs were each about 8 inches (20 cm) long.

Egg of Protoceratops

Bird egg

Do we know what they ate?

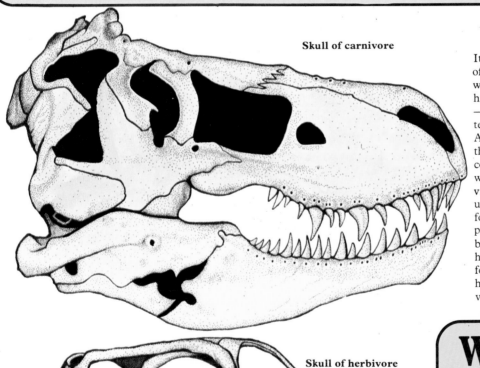

Skull of carnivore

It has been relatively easy to discover which of the dinosaurs were meat-eaters and which were plant-eaters. The meat-eaters had well-developed—often very powerful —jaws, and had sharp teeth with which to tear flesh from their prey and chew it. Also, they were built as hunters. Either they were very speedy—and, as a result, could catch their prey easily—or they were extremely strong and were armed with vicious claws and talons. The plant-eaters usually had teeth adapted to grinding their food. In some cases, it is clear that a particular dinosaur was a plant-eater because the front of its jaw projected in a horny beak. This would have been useless for eating meat, but would have been very helpful in reaching and cutting tough vegetation.

Skull of herbivore

Were they warm blooded?

Some experts have said that dinosaurs may have been warm blooded. But it is unlikely that they were warm blooded throughout their lives in the way that mammals and birds are. These creatures absorb their food very quickly, and their bodies are insulated by fur or feathers and retain heat. Dinosaurs had scaly outer coverings. If they were warm blooded, they would have needed to eat every second of the day in order to obtain a sufficiently large food intake.

THE LIZARD-HIPPED ONES The saurischians—or lizard-hipped—dinosaurs included both meat-eaters and plant-eaters. There were several different groups of them, including the very large and slow-moving sauropods, and the vicious theropods. The sauropods walked on all fours, and were plant-eaters. They reached the peak of their development during Jurassic times, though in the Southern Hemisphere they survived until the end of the Cretaceous period. They were of low intelligence. They probably died out because they were unable to adapt to changes in their environment. The theropods, walking on their hind legs, preyed on plant-eating dinosaurs and other timid creatures. One kind, the coelurosaurs, relied on speed to catch their victims. The carnosaurs used their strength.

How did the saurischia and ornithischia differ?

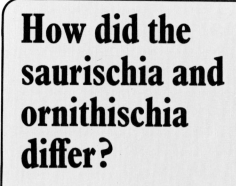

Ornithischian (Triceratops)

Saurischian (Tyrannosaurus)

The major difference between the two groups of dinosaurs is the arrangement of the hip bones. In the lizard-hipped dinosaurs (saurischians), the front part of the pelvis is directed downward and forward. In the bird-hipped dinosaurs (ornithischians), it points downward and backward.

How many kinds of saurischia were there?

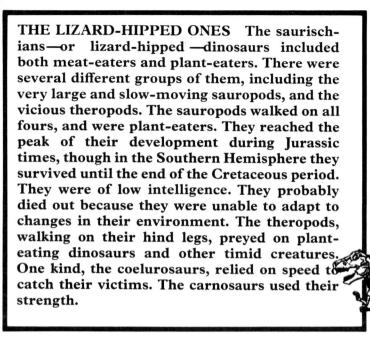

Coelurosaur
(Ornithomimus)

The lizard-hipped dinosaurs included animals that were very unlike each other in appearance and that had different ways of life. Among them were the fast-moving coelurosaurs, the vicious carnosaurs, and the clumsy, plant-eating sauropods.

Carnosaur (Allosaurus)

Sauropod (Diplodocus)

What was the first dinosaur named?

The first dinosaur named was the large, flesh-eating *Megalosaurus*, which lived in Jurassic times. Though it was not identified until 1824, it had been known for a long time. A bone of a creature that may have been *Megalosaurus* was pictured in a book published in the 1600's. At that time, people thought that it was the remains of a gigantic human.

Megalosaurus

What was the biggest?

The largest of all the dinosaurs was *Brachiosaurus*. It was the biggest land animal that ever existed. The heaviest examples may have weighed over 100 tons. One *Brachiosaurus* whose remains have been found was 98 feet (30 meters) long. Its head was 39 feet (12 meters) from the ground. Brachiosaurus lived in swampy regions in North America and Africa during Jurassic times. Although a land animal, it was able to move more easily in water, where its vast body was better supported.

Brachiosaurus

Tyrannosaurus

What was the fiercest?

The fiercest dinosaur seems to have been *Tyrannosaurus*. Its name means "tyrant lizard." It stood nearly 13 feet (4 meters) tall, and was about 50 feet (15 meters) long. Its teeth were as long as a pencil. It had terrible claws, which it used to grasp and tear its prey. Fossils of *Tyrannosaurus* have been found in North America and Asia.

Were the ornithischians all the same?

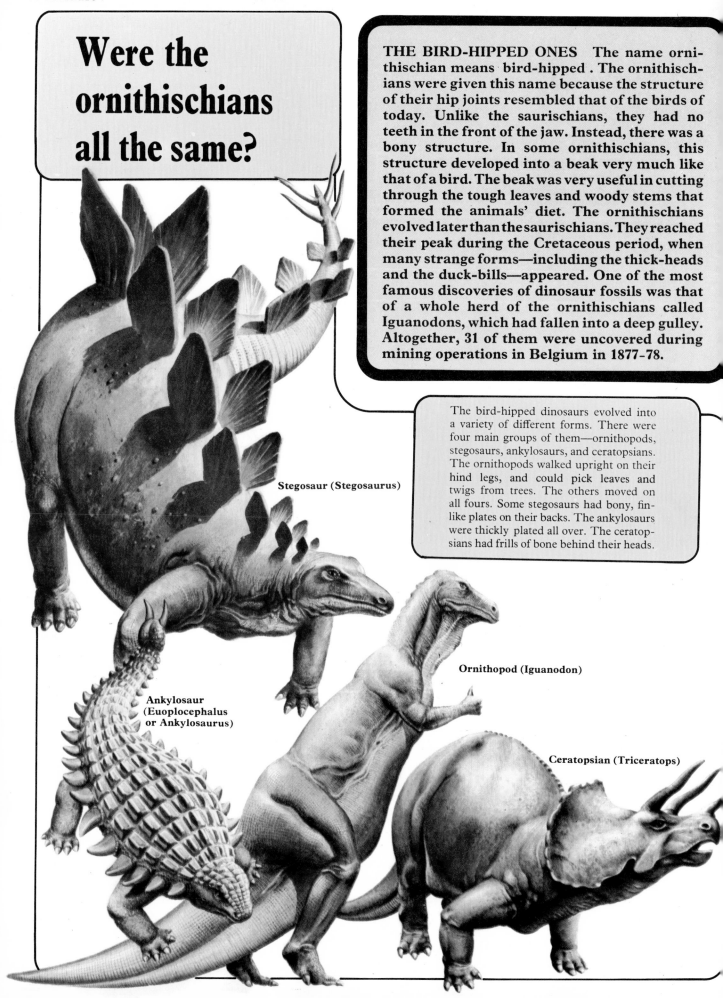

THE BIRD-HIPPED ONES The name ornithischian means bird-hipped . The ornithischians were given this name because the structure of their hip joints resembled that of the birds of today. Unlike the saurischians, they had no teeth in the front of the jaw. Instead, there was a bony structure. In some ornithischians, this structure developed into a beak very much like that of a bird. The beak was very useful in cutting through the tough leaves and woody stems that formed the animals' diet. The ornithischians evolved later than the saurischians. They reached their peak during the Cretaceous period, when many strange forms—including the thick-heads and the duck-bills—appeared. One of the most famous discoveries of dinosaur fossils was that of a whole herd of the ornithischians called Iguanodons, which had fallen into a deep gulley. Altogether, 31 of them were uncovered during mining operations in Belgium in 1877-78.

The bird-hipped dinosaurs evolved into a variety of different forms. There were four main groups of them—ornithopods, stegosaurs, ankylosaurs, and ceratopsians. The ornithopods walked upright on their hind legs, and could pick leaves and twigs from trees. The others moved on all fours. Some stegosaurs had bony, fin-like plates on their backs. The ankylosaurs were thickly plated all over. The ceratopsians had frills of bone behind their heads.

Stegosaur (Stegosaurus)

Ankylosaur
(Euoplocephalus
or Ankylosaurus)

Ornithopod (Iguanodon)

Ceratopsian (Triceratops)

Did they have any other bird characteristics?

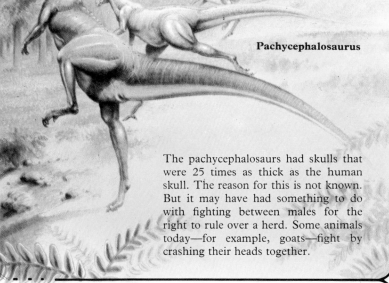

Anatosaurus

The hadrosaurs had another bird-like characteristic apart from their hip joints. The front part of the hadrosaur's face was flattened, and projected to form a bill like that of a duck. But this bill sometimes contained more than 2,000 teeth. The hadrosaurs were able to live both on land and in the water.

Why are some of them called "thick-headed"?

Pachycephalosaurus

The pachycephalosaurs had skulls that were 25 times as thick as the human skull. The reason for this is not known. But it may have had something to do with fighting between males for the right to rule over a herd. Some animals today—for example, goats—fight by crashing their heads together.

How big were their brains?

Nerve center

Brain

Nearly all the dinosaurs had small brains. Some of the largest had brains that were only as big as a hen's egg. At one time it was thought that some dinosaurs had a second brain in the hip. But this supposed brain is only a nerve center.

What kind of plants did they eat?

Leptoceratops

There were great changes in both the numbers and the types of plants during the age of the dinosaurs. In Triassic times, there were relatively few land plants. But by the end of the Cretaceous period, the vegetation looked much like that of today. It was during this period that the first flowering plants appeared. Conifers, cycads, and ferns were common.

How did the pterosaurs evolve?

The pterosaurs were certainly reptiles. But scientists can only guess how the reptiles—who had moved onto land from the seas—eventually took to the air. It is possible that some early tree-living dinosaurs grew skin webs between their limbs that helped them to jump from branch to branch. In time, they were able to glide—at first over short distances, and then over longer distances. Some modern tree-living lizards have webs of this kind. The later pterosaurs had strong joints between backbone and wings.

THE FLYING REPTILES During the Jurassic and Cretaceous periods, strange shapes were seen in the sky as well as on land and in the seas. The reptiles had taken to the air. For more than 100 million years, leathery-winged pterosaurs swooped and glided overhead in a ceaseless search for food.

Pterosaur

Flying lizard

Did they look like birds?

Rhamphorhynchus

All pterosaurs had small bodies, though some had huge wings. Some of the early forms had teeth, and many had long tails. *Pteranodons* had no teeth, but had long, heavy jaws and bony crests on their heads.

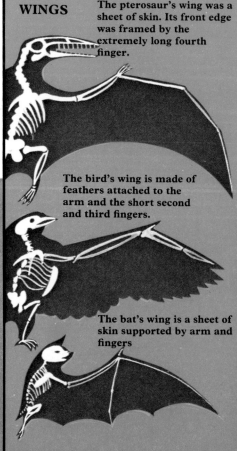

WINGS The pterosaur's wing was a sheet of skin. Its front edge was framed by the extremely long fourth finger.

The bird's wing is made of feathers attached to the arm and the short second and third fingers.

The bat's wing is a sheet of skin supported by arm and fingers

Crested Head

It is thought that *Pteranodon's* long crest held its head straight when flying.

How big were they?

Some pterosaurs were only as big as a blackbird. But *Pteranodon* was the largest flying creature of all time. It had a wing span of about 25 feet (8 meters).

Pteranodon

How well could they fly?

Many pterosaurs had small feet that were probably too weak to support them. They would not have been able to walk or to take off from the ground. They may have thrown themselves into the air from cliffs or trees. Their wings were not well designed for flying, and they probably traveled through the air by soaring and gliding.

Where did they live?

North America

Europe

Asia

Africa

Pterosaurs seem to have lived in most parts of the world as it was in their time. Their remains have been found in many places in most of the continents.

Where did the first bird come from?

The earliest bird that we know about lived some 150 million years ago. It is called *Archaeopteryx*. It was about the size of a pigeon, and evolved from reptilian ancestors. Some scientists believe that birds are descended from the small coelurosaur dinosaurs, of which *Compsognathus* is an example.

THE FIRST BIRDS Birds are not the only animals to have become successful flyers. The great flying reptiles mastered the air in pre-historic times. Bats, which are mammals, spend much of their time in the air. And so do insects, which are invertebrates. Birds are in many ways like reptiles. But they also have important differences from them. These differences result from the way birds live.

Archaeopteryx

How do we know about it?

The first *Archaeopteryx* fossil was discovered in a quarry at Solnhofen, in Bavaria, Germany. It was found in fine-grained stone that showed up details. As a result, scientists could clearly see the impressions of feathers. Otherwise, they would have thought that the fossil was that of a reptile. Other fossils have since been found.

Archaeopteryx fossil

Was it like the birds of today?

Archaeopteryx had feathers that were arranged in the same way as those of the birds of today. That is, there were nine primary and fourteen secondary feathers. And, like modern birds, it was able to perch. But it also had a number of reptilian features. For example, it had teeth.

The skull of *Archaeopteryx* resembled that of a reptile. Clawed toes on its wings may have been used in climbing.

How well could it fly?

What other early birds do we know about?

Archaeopteryx was not a very successful flyer. Its breastbone—unlike that of a modern bird—was small, and did not provide a large enough area for the attachment of strong flying muscles. It probably spent its life jumping from branch to branch and gliding.

Ichthyornis

Diatryma

Archaeopteryx is the only known bird of the Jurassic period. A few are known from the Cretaceous period. They include *Hesperornis*, a toothed, flightless, water-living bird, about 3 feet (1 meter) long. Another was *Ichthyornis*, which was somewhat like a modern gull. The fossils of several giant birds have been discovered. One of them is *Diatryma*, a flightless bird about 6 feet (2 meters) high.

Hesperornis

EVOLUTION

Fossils of birds are rarely found, and, as a result, it is difficult to trace the bird's evolution. By about 60 million years ago, at least half of the kinds of birds known today had already evolved. And, of course, several kinds of birds have already become extinct. They include many of the giant birds that once lived in the Southern Hemisphere.

What reptiles lived in the sea?

REPTILES OF THE SEA Just as the great reptiles called dinosaurs developed into many different forms on land, other reptiles became the dominant creatures in the sea. Some groups, such as the fish-eating nothosaurs and the shell-fish-eating placodonts, lived only in the Triassic period. Others, including the ichthyosaurs, showed little change during 130 million years. Many sea reptiles died out with the dinosaurs. But the descendants of others are still alive today.

The best-known of the sea-living reptiles are the ichthyosaurs and plesiosaurs. The ichthyosaurs spent all their lives at sea. They did not come ashore to lay their eggs, and their young were born alive. The plesiosaurs were able to move clumsily on land. Other reptiles included the mosasaurs and the chelonians—turtles and tortoises.

Ichthyosaurs spent all their lives at sea.

Turtles, like plesiosaurs, were land and water animals.

Plesiosaurs lived both on land and in the water.

Mosasaurs were large water-living lizards.

How did reptiles swim?

The streamlined, dolphin-like ichthyosaurs were well adapted to life in the sea. They could swim very fast, using their bodies and tails as fishes do. Their paddles helped them to steer. The plesiosaurs used their powerful paddles to row themselves along. They could not swim as well as the ichthyosaurs, and they rarely went below the surface waters.

Ichthyosaurs

Plesiosaurs

What did they eat?

The sea reptiles ate many kinds of food, including shellfish, fish, and ammonites. But they did not all have the same diet. The ichthyosaurs had sharp teeth, and they lived on fish and ammonites. The placodonts—which lived at an earlier period—had crushing teeth that enabled them to break open shellfish. Some of the plesiosaurs had very powerful jaws. Their food may have included other reptiles.

A Dedicated Collector

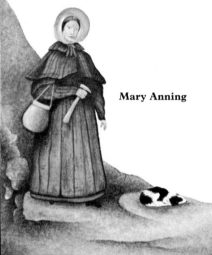

Mary Anning

Mary Anning (1799–1847) was the first person to discover ichthyosaur, plesiosaur, and pterosaur skeletons. She spent all her life in Lyme Regis, in Dorset in England, and—like her father—made a living by collecting and selling fossils. Some of her discoveries were made while she was a child. The Dorset coast is one of a number of places—in various parts of the world—famous for fossils.

How are the various kinds of reptiles related?

The sea reptiles evolved along many lines. The earliest reptiles of all lived about 300 million years ago. The chelonians first appeared in Permian times, and the earliest-known land tortoise dates back about 215 million years. One large group of sea reptiles includes the nothosaurs and placodonts, which lived only in Triassic times. It also includes the plesiosaurs, which flourished during the Jurassic and Cretaceous periods. The ichthyosaurs form a separate family. Other reptile groups had some sea-living animals among their members. Mosasaurs, for example, were sea-living lizards. The only archosaurs to take to the sea were a group of crocodiles that are now extinct.

Did dinosaurs evolve before mammals?

THE DINOSAURS' WORLD The world in which the dinosaurs lived was very different from the world we know. During their long reign, there were many changes. The continents drifted apart, climates altered, and new animals and plants appeared. Various new kinds of dinosaurs evolved as a result of changes in the environment. Other kinds died out long before the extinction of the whole group at the end of the Cretaceous period.

Dimetrodon was a pelycosaur. Triconodon was a mammal.

The pelycosaur Dimetrodon was related to the ancestors of the mammals. Its "sail" probably absorbed heat from the sun.

The first mammals evolved during the Triassic period. Their line of evolution went back to the pelycosaurs of Carboniferous and Permian times. Though mammals lived on Earth during the whole of the reign of the dinosaurs, they remained small and insignificant. They probably hid under low plants during the daytime, and became active only at night.

What plants grew?

DIMETRODON

TRICONODON

In Triassic times, few plants grew. Cycads and tree-ferns became common in the Jurassic period. The ginkgo tree was widespread. In the Cretaceous period, modern flowering plants evolved. By the end of the period, plants looked very much like those of today.

Ginkgo or maidenhair tree. It still grows today.

The primitive mammal Triconodon evolved at the end of the Triassic period. It was probably carnivorous and had a hairy coat.

Did dinosaurs evolve before insects?

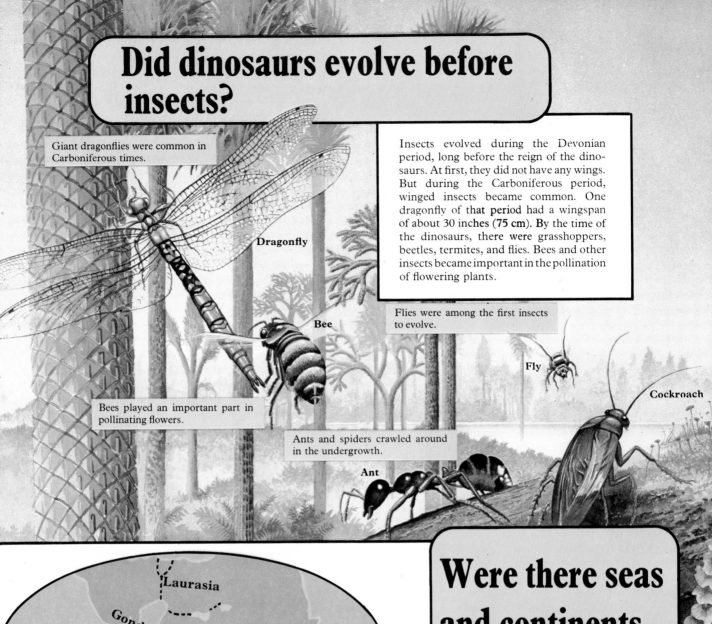

Giant dragonflies were common in Carboniferous times.

Dragonfly

Insects evolved during the Devonian period, long before the reign of the dinosaurs. At first, they did not have any wings. But during the Carboniferous period, winged insects became common. One dragonfly of that period had a wingspan of about 30 inches (75 cm). By the time of the dinosaurs, there were grasshoppers, beetles, termites, and flies. Bees and other insects became important in the pollination of flowering plants.

Bee

Flies were among the first insects to evolve.

Fly

Cockroach

Bees played an important part in pollinating flowers.

Ants and spiders crawled around in the undergrowth.

Ant

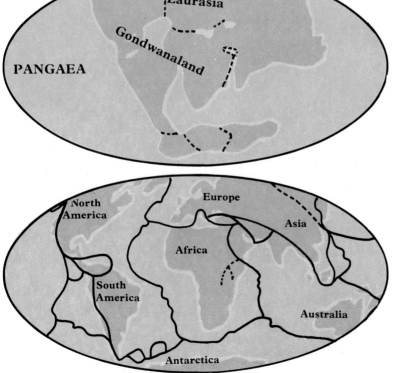

Laurasia

Gondwanaland

PANGAEA

North America

Europe

Asia

Africa

South America

Australia

Antarctica

Were there seas and continents as we know them?

Before the time of the dinosaurs, the world's continents had formed a huge, single land mass called *Pangaea*. Then, Pangaea began to split up. By the end of the Triassic period, the northern group of continents had drifted away from the southern group. When the Cretaceous period ended, many of the continents were much as we know them today.

What were the last dinosaurs?

THE END OF AN ERA Toward the end of the Cretaceous period, the long reign of the dinosaurs came to an end. No dinosaur fossils have been found in any rocks deposited after the end of the period. Dinosaurs had been the lords of the Earth for some 150 million years. They had evolved a great variety of forms and had managed to live in almost every kind of environment.

Anatosaurus

Alamosaurus

Parasaurolophus

In the later part of the Cretaceous period, trees and other plants had evolved that were much like those we know today. We would have recognized the woods of oaks, maples, and chestnuts. But we would have been surprised by the wildlife. It included some of the strangest of the dinosaurs, including the sauropod *Alamosaurus*, and the hadrosaurs *Anatosaurus* and *Parasaurolophus*.

Who ruled the world after the dinosaurs?

For a long time, the mammals had been overshadowed by the great reptiles. Now they took over the world. They included animals as varied as the dull creodont, the timid eohippus, the ferocious sabre-toothed cat—and human beings and the creatures of their world.

Creodont

Eohippus

Sabre-toothed cat

Have many other kinds of animals become extinct?

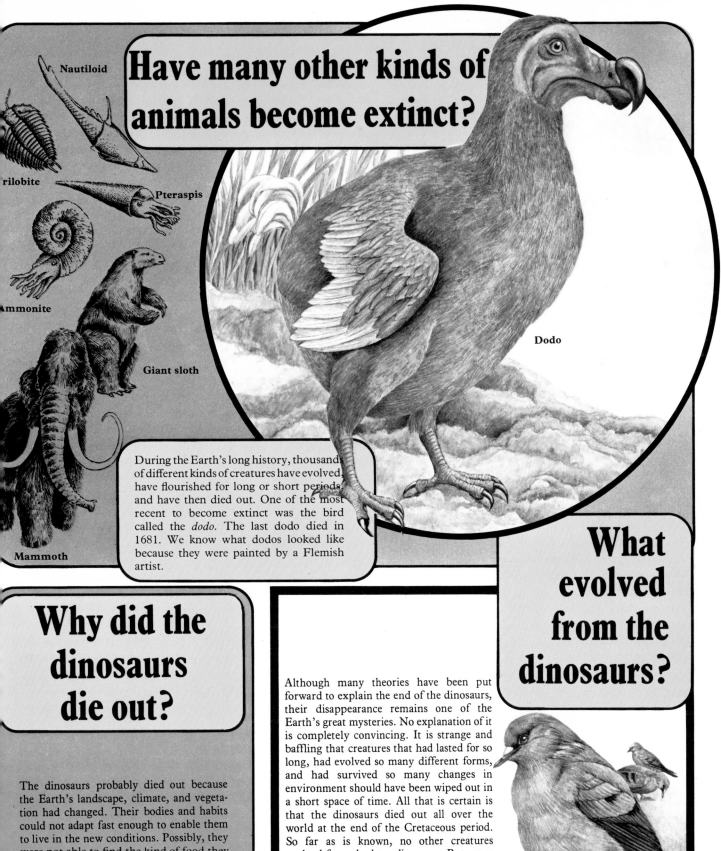

Nautiloid

Trilobite

Pteraspis

Ammonite

Giant sloth

Mammoth

Dodo

During the Earth's long history, thousands of different kinds of creatures have evolved, have flourished for long or short periods, and have then died out. One of the most recent to become extinct was the bird called the *dodo*. The last dodo died in 1681. We know what dodos looked like because they were painted by a Flemish artist.

What evolved from the dinosaurs?

Why did the dinosaurs die out?

The dinosaurs probably died out because the Earth's landscape, climate, and vegetation had changed. Their bodies and habits could not adapt fast enough to enable them to live in the new conditions. Possibly, they were not able to find the kind of food they needed. As many parts of the world became cooler, they may have been unable to withstand the cold. They may also have been harmed by winds and drought, or even by radiation from space.

Although many theories have been put forward to explain the end of the dinosaurs, their disappearance remains one of the Earth's great mysteries. No explanation of it is completely convincing. It is strange and baffling that creatures that had lasted for so long, had evolved so many different forms, and had survived so many changes in environment should have been wiped out in a short space of time. All that is certain is that the dinosaurs died out all over the world at the end of the Cretaceous period. So far as is known, no other creatures evolved from the later dinosaurs. But many scientists believe that birds are descended from the early coelurosaurs, who belonged to the theropod (beast-footed) group. The modern robin, sparrow, or pigeon, pecking crumbs in a city park, may have in it the blood of the mighty reptiles that once ruled the world.

Where can we see dinosaurs today?

Dinosaurs became extinct long before humans inhabited the Earth, and little remains of these strange creatures today except their bones. These bones are carefully put together to re-create the animals' skeletons. Such skeletons can be seen in many museums, though they are not always the skeletons of the great monsters. Models of how the animals looked in life are made by experts, and shown with the bones.

LOOKING FOR DINOSAURS Remains of dinosaurs have been found in every continent except Antarctica. Many of the best dinosaur fossils have come from what are today the remoter parts of the world—for example, from Mongolia. The first expeditions to look for fossils were organized in the 1800's. Often, there was fierce competition between early collectors, who seemed to be racing each other to discover new kinds of prehistoric creatures. The finding of more and more specimens helps scientists to make accurate reconstructions. When scientists made the first model of Iguanodon, they showed it walking on all fours and with a horn on its nose. Later discoveries proved that Iguanodon walked on its hind legs, and that the "horn" was really part of its thumb.

How have their remains been found?

Many finds of dinosaur fossils have been accidental. The remains have been exposed because of a cliff fall, or when workmen were quarrying or digging foundations for roads or buildings. Once a particular area is known to contain dinosaur fossils, scientists may arrange for a scientific expedition to the spot to make sure that this valuable evidence of life in past ages is not spoiled or lost. Such expeditions have traveled to all parts of the world.

Is it difficult to dig them out?

The job of excavating a fossil is usu[a] slow and tedious. A whole skeleton m[ay] be buried deep in rock. But if it is to be [of] value, every fragment must be collect[ed]. This requires both skill and patience.

How is a dinosaur "reborn"?

When the bones have been removed from the rock, they are carefully joined together to build up a complete skeleton. The work is somewhat like a huge jigsaw puzzle in which some of the pieces may be missing. Gradually, the expert can build up a model showing what the dinosaur looked like.

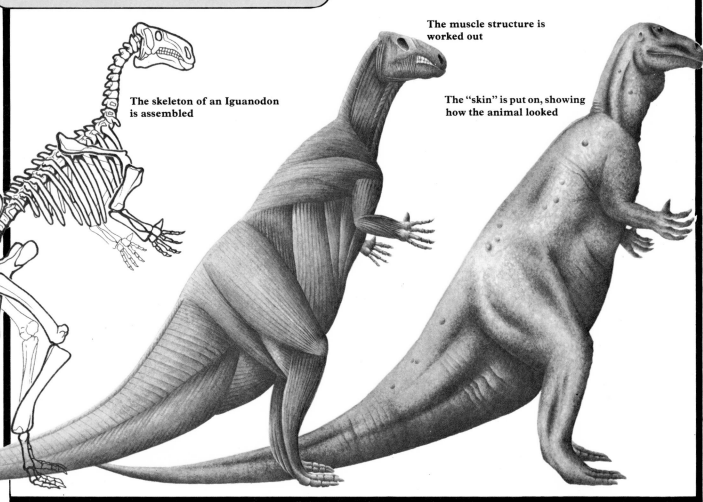

The skeleton of an Iguanodon is assembled

The muscle structure is worked out

The "skin" is put on, showing how the animal looked

What work do scientists do on them?

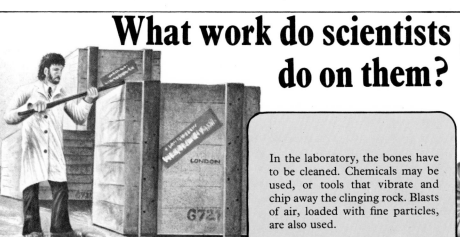

In the laboratory, the bones have to be cleaned. Chemicals may be used, or tools that vibrate and chip away the clinging rock. Blasts of air, loaded with fine particles, are also used.

Dinosaur Spotter

Diplodocus
(90 feet; 28 meters)

Tyrannosaurus
(50 feet; 15 meters)

Stegosaurus (30 feet; 9 meters)

Compsognathus (12 inches; 30 cm)

Hypsilophodon (6 feet; 2 meters)

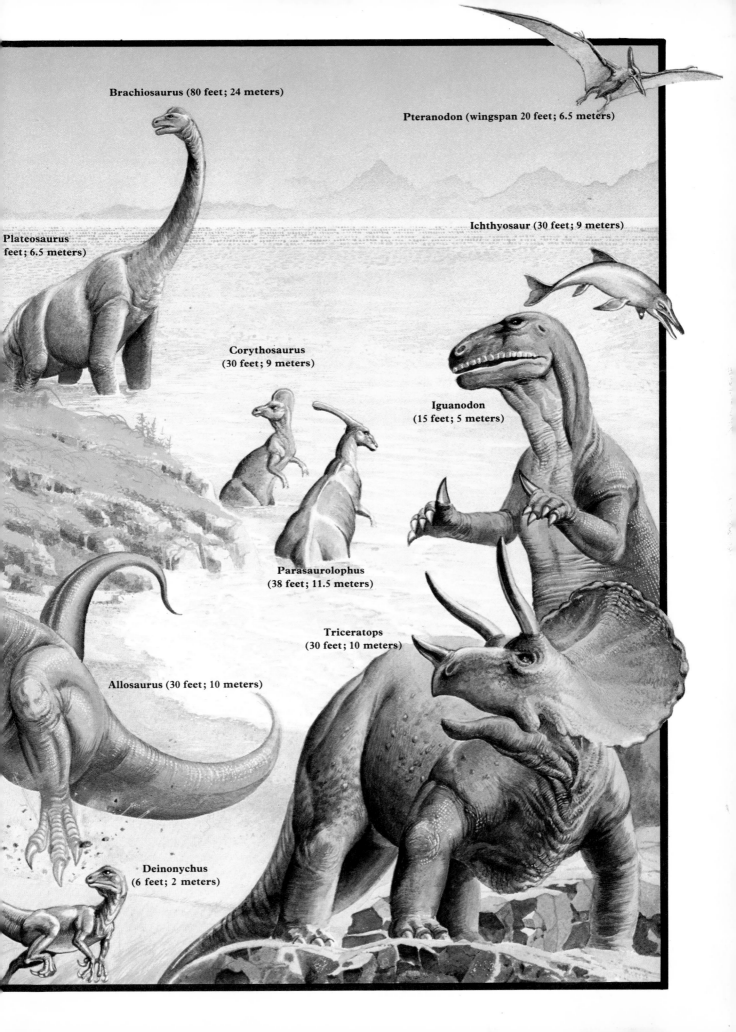

Brachiosaurus (80 feet; 24 meters)

Pteranodon (wingspan 20 feet; 6.5 meters)

Ichthyosaur (30 feet; 9 meters)

Plateosaurus
feet; 6.5 meters)

Corythosaurus
(30 feet; 9 meters)

Iguanodon
(15 feet; 5 meters)

Parasaurolophus
(38 feet; 11.5 meters)

Triceratops
(30 feet; 10 meters)

Allosaurus (30 feet; 10 meters)

Deinonychus
(6 feet; 2 meters)

A-Z of Dinosaurs

A

Allosaurus *al oh SAWR us* A Jurassic carnosaur that was about 30 feet (10 meters) long and lived in North America. It was a bipedal meat-eater.

Anatosaurus *an at oh SAWR us* A duck-billed dinosaur that lived at the very end of the Cretaceous period. Unlike some of the other hadrosaurs, it did not have a crest on its head.

ankylosaurs *an KY lo sawrs* One of the major groups of ornithischian dinosaurs. They moved on all fours, and had a tank-like body.

Apatosaurus *uh pat oh SAWR us* Formerly called *Brontosaurus*, it was a giant sauropod about 80 feet (25 meters) long and weighed up to 30 tons. It lived in swamp lands.

BC

Brachiosaurus *bracky oh SAWR us* ("arm lizard") The largest land animal that ever lived. This sauropod weighed 80 tons, and its head was about 45 feet (13 meters) from the ground. It lived in late Jurassic times in Africa and the U.S.A.

Brontosaurus *See* APATOSAURUS.

carnosaurs *CAR no sawrs* A group of bipedal meat-eating dinosaurs that includes Allosaurus and Tyrannosaurus.

ceratopsians *ser uh TOP see ans* A group of plant-eating ornithischian dinosaurs that includes Protoceratops and Triceratops.

Coelophysis *see lo FY sis* ("hollow form") An early coelurosaur that lived in Triassic times. It was about 8 feet (2.5 meters) long and was bipedal.

coelurosaurs *see LOOR oh sawrs* A group of bipedal, meat-eating saurischians that includes Deinonychus, Coelophysis, and Ornithomimus.

Compsognathus *comp so NAY thus* The smallest of the dinosaurs, about 12 inches (30 cm) long. It was a bipedal meat-eater that lived in Jurassic times.

Corythosaurus *co rith oh SAWR us* ("helmet lizard") A hadrosaur that lived in North America during Upper Cretaceous times. It had webbed fingers and a hollow crest over its head.

D

Deinonychus *dine oh NY kus* ("terrible claw") A carnosaur that lived in Cretaceous times. Although relatively small—about 6 feet (2 meters) long—it had a sickle-shaped claw on each of its hind feet which it used to tear at its prey.

dinosaur *DINE oh sawr* ("terrible lizard") The name suggested in 1841 by Professor Richard Owen for a group of extinct reptiles that lived from Triassic to Cretaceous times.

Diplodocus *di PLOD oh kus* The longest of the dinosaurs. It was a sauropod that lived in the Jurassic swamps. It was about 90 feet (28 meters) long and weighed about 10 tons.

duck-billed dinosaurs *See* HADROSAURS.

FHIM

Fabrosaurus *fab roh SAWR us* An early ornithischian. It was about 3 feet (1 meter) long. Although it spent much of its time on all fours, it was capable of running on its hind legs.

hadrosaurs *HAD roh sawrs* A group of ornithopods. They were very successful during Cretaceous times. A number of different forms evolved. The jaws and teeth became well adapted to eating tough plant material. Some developed crests that were up to 6 feet (2 meters) in length.

Hypsilophodon *hip sil OFF oh don* ("high ridge tooth") An ornithopod that lived in the early Cretaceous time and grew to a length of about 6 feet (2 meters). It had a horny beak.

Iguanodon *ig WAN oh don* ("Iguana" and "tooth") Bipedal ornithopod that lived in early Cretaceous times, and was about 15 feet (5 meters) tall. It was the second dinosaur to be given a name.

Megalosaurus *meg al oh SAWR us* ("big lizard") A bipedal carnosaur that lived in Europe in Jurassic times. It was the first dinosaur named. It was about 20 feet (6.5 meters) long, and weighed about 2 tons.

OP

ornithischians *or nith ISK ee ans* One of the two great groups of dinosaurs. The ornithischians—the bird-hipped dinosaurs—included the ornithopods, stegosaurs, ceratopsians, and ankylosaurs.

Ornitholestes *or nith oh LESS tees* A fast-moving Jurassic coelurosaur. It was about 6 feet (2 meters) long.

Ornithomimus *or nith oh MY mus* ("bird imitator") Coelurosaur that lived in Asia and North America in Cretaceous times. It was about 13 feet (4 meters) long.

ornithopods *or NITH oh pods* The major group of the plant-eating ornithischians. It includes Hypsilophodon and Iguanodon.

Ornithosuchus *or nith oh SOOK us* The earliest dinosaur. A bipedal flesh-eating animal, it grew to a length of about 10 feet (3 meters). The great carnosaurs Allosaurus and Tyrannosaurus were its descendants.

Pachycephalosaurus *packy sef al oh SAWR us* ("thick-headed lizard") One of the bone-headed dinosaurs, so called because of the thickness of its skull.

Plateosaurus *plat ee oh SAWR us* ("flat lizard") A sauropod that lived in late Triassic times. It was about 29 feet (6.4 meters) long.

Polacanthus *pol uh CAN thus* ("many-spined") A tank-like ankylosaur, about 13 feet (4 meters) long, that lived in early Cretaceous times. It had two rows of spines along its back.

Protoceratops *pro toh SER uh tops* ("first horned face") An early ceratopsian that, in spite of its name, did not have a horn. It moved on all fours, and had a bony frill around the back of its neck. Remains have been found in Mongolia in rocks of Upper Cretaceous age. Nests of its eggs have also been discovered.

S

saurischians *sawr ISK ee ans* One of the two major groups of dinosaurs. They included the plant-eating sauropods and the meat-eating theropods.

sauropods *SAWR oh pods* ("reptile feet") One of the two major groups of the saurischian dinosaurs. They included such giants as Brachiosaurus. All were plant-eaters.

Scelidosaurus *skel ee doh SAWR us* ("limb lizard") An early ornithischian that moved on all fours. It was just under 13 feet (4 meters) long, and its back was armor plated.

Stegosaurus *steg oh SAWR us* ("roof lizard") About 20–30 feet (6–9 meters) long, Stegosaurus has been found in North America in rocks of Jurassic age. It is usually pictured as having two great rows of plates along its back. In most pictures, these are upright, but some scientists suggest that they should project sideways.

T

theropods *THER oh pods* ("beast feet") One of the two major groups of saurischian dinosaurs. They include the flesh-eating coelurosaurs and carnosaurs.

Triceratops *try SER uh tops* ("three horned face") A ceratopsian that lived in herds in North America during late Cretaceous times. It had a horn on its nose and one above each eye. Like Protoceratops, it had a small frill of bone over the neck.

Tyrannosaurus *tir an oh SAWR us* ("tyrant lizard") The largest and most ferocious of the flesh-eating dinosaurs. Its remains have been found in rocks of Cretaceous age in North America and Asia. It stood about 15 feet (5 meters) tall, and weighed about 7 tons.

Quick Reference: The Prehistoric World

A

Aepyornis *ay pee OR nis* ("high bird") Flightless birds that lived until very recent times on the island of Madagascar. The tallest was about 10 feet (3 meters) high.

ammonites *AM on ites* Invertebrate sea-living animals related to the squid. Their coiled shells are often found as fossils. The one living member of the group is the pearly nautilus.

amphibian One of the major groups of vertebrate animals. They are still dependent on the water, to which they return to lay their eggs. The group includes frogs, newts and salamanders.

anatomy The study of the structure of plants and animals.

angiosperms One of the great divisions of the seed-bearing plants. It includes all the higher flowering plants, which evolved in Cretaceous times. The seeds develop within an enclosed seed vessel.

Archaeopteryx *ar kee OP ter icks* ("ancient wing") The earliest bird so far discovered. Found in the lithographic limestone of Bavaria, in Germany. This bird of the Jurassic period had many reptilian features, including teeth.

Archelon *ar KEL on* A giant turtle which was about 13 feet (4 meters) long, and lived in Cretaceous times.

archosaurs *AR ko sawrs* A group of animals that includes the dinosaurs, crocodiles, and flying reptiles. Strictly speaking, it should also include the birds, but these are now treated as a separate group.

articulated skeleton A fossil skeleton in which the bones are still joined as when the creature was alive.

B

backbone The vertebral column of the vertebrate animals. It is made up of varying-sized blocks of bone, called *vertebrae*. These are separated by disks of cartilage.

bipedal An animal that walks on two feet in a semi-upright or upright posture.

bird-hipped The arrangement of bones in the hip in which the pubis points backward and downward parallel to the ischium. One of the major groups of dinosaurs are the ornithischians—the bird-hipped dinosaurs.

brain The control center of the nervous system.

C

carnivore A meat-eating animal. The word is also used as *Carnivora* for an order of mammals.

chelonians *ke LOHN ee ans* A group of reptiles that includes the tortoises, turtles, and terrapins.

cold-blooded Animals whose body-heat changes with changes in the temperature of the outside air.

conifers Evergreen trees that produce cones.

continental drift The gradual movement of the continents away from the one great land-mass called *Pangaea*.

cycads A class of cone-bearing plants that were very common in Mesozoic times, when they grew to the size of trees.

Cynognathus *sy nog NATH us* ("dog jaw") A mammal-like reptile that lived in early Triassic times.

D

Diatryma *dy uh TRY ma* A giant flightless bird that lived in Eocene times, and stood about 6.5 feet (2 meters) high. It had a very powerful beak.

Dimetrodon *dy MET ro don* ("double-size tooth") An early mammal-like reptile, characterized by the "sail" along its back. It lived in early Permian times.

E

environment The natural or artificial conditions affecting a plant or animal.

Euparkeria *yew park EER ee ah* A small archosaur about 3 feet (1 meter) long. It was an ancestor of the dinosaurs.

evolution The gradual development of more complex forms of plant and animal life from relatively generalized forms.

extinct Animals and plants that have no living representatives.

F

flying reptiles *See* PTEROSAURS.

footprints The fossil impressions of tracks. They were originally made in soft mud. This later became rock.

fossilization The process of preservation of animals and plants, and of signs of their activity.

fossils The remains of animals and plants of past eras, or the traces of their activity.

G

genus (plural *genera*) A division of an animal or plant *family*. It is made up of a number of *species*.

geology The science of the Earth, its development, structure, and history, and the materials of which it is made.

geosaurus *jee oh SAWR us* A marine crocodile which lived in the Jurassic seas. It was about 16 feet (5 meters) long.

ginkgo An order of cone-bearing trees, of which the maidenhair tree is the sole survivor.

H

habitat The condition existing where a plant or animal lives. *See* ENVIRONMENT.

herbivore A plant-eating animal.

Hesperornis *hess per AWR nis* ("western bird") A flightless, toothed Cretaceous diving bird about 6.5 feet (2 meters) long.

Hylonomus *hi LON oh mus* A very early reptile living in late Carboniferous times.

I

Ichthyornis *ick thee OR nis* ("fish bird") A tern-like bird about 8 inches (20 cm) long which lived in late Cretaceous times.

ichthyosaurs *ICK thee oh sawrs* A group of sea-living reptiles particularly common in the Jurassic period.

invertebrates Animals without a backbone.

L

laboratory The part of a museum or similar organization that treats specimens and attempts to preserve them. It may also undertake cleaning and mounting for display.

lizard-hipped The arrangement of bones in the hip in which the pubis is directed downward and forward and the ischium below and behind. One of the major divisions of the dinosaurs are the saurischians—the lizard-hipped dinosaurs.

Lystrosaurus *liss troh SAWR us* ("shovel lizard") A plant-eating, mammal-like reptile. It was about 10 feet (3 meters) long and existed in Permian and Triassic times. It lived partly on land and partly in water.

M

mammal A warm-blooded, backboned animal. The young are born alive and are suckled by the mother. Mammals usually have fur.

mammal-like reptiles A group of reptiles with mammal-like characteristics. The true mammals evolved from them. They lived in Triassic and Jurassic times.

metabolic rate The rate at which food is converted into energy. Warm-blooded animals—mammals and birds—have a high metabolic rate.

Mixosaurus *mix oh SAWR us* An early ichthyosaur.

mossaurs *mos SAWRS* (from River Maas and "lizard") Aquatic-living lizards of late Cretaceous times, some of which grew to nearly 30 feet (10 meters) in length.

nothosaurs *NOTH oh sawrs* A group of Triassic reptiles that could live both in the water and on land. They had long tails and relatively short necks.

names, scientific Each individual animal and plant has two Latin names, which denote the genus and species, for example *Tyrannosaurus rex*.

O P

omnivore An animal that satisfies its food needs by eating both plants and animals.

paleontology The science of the study of fossils. Its purpose is to create a history of life on the Earth from the earliest geologic time to the present.

Pangaea The original super-continent. It began to break up in Mesozoic times into the continents as they now exist.

pelvic girdle The hip bones.

pelycosaurs *PEL ee ko sawrs* A group of early reptiles that lived in late Carboniferous and Permian times. Many developed a sail-like structure on their backs. Dimetrodon was a pelycosaur.

Phororhacos *for or ACK us* ("bearing wrinkles") A flightless bird that lived in South America in Miocene times. It was about 5 feet (1.5 meters) tall.

placodonts *PLACK oh donts* Triassic reptiles with an armored back, and teeth that were adapted for crushing shellfish. They lived in water.

plesiosaurs *plees ee oh SAWRS* A group of sea-living reptiles that lived during Jurassic and Cretaceous times. They were not as well adapted to the water as were the ichthyosaurs. The pliosaurs had shorter necks and more powerful heads than the other plesiosaurs.

pterosaurs *TER oh sawrs* The flying reptiles that included *Rhamphorhynchus* ("beak snout"), a Jurassic form, and *Pteranodon* ("wing without teeth"), a Cretaceous pterodactyl. Pterosaurs were the first vertebrates to take to the air.

Q R S

quadruped An animal that moves on all fours.

reptile A cold-blooded vertebrate animal that has scales and lays its eggs on land.

saurian *SAWR ee an* A very general name applied to animals, especially reptiles, that have a number of lizard-like characteristics.

skeleton The structural bone framework of a vertebrate animal.

species The division of a *genus*, and the smallest group that can breed and have fertile offspring.

T

taxonomy The science of classifying animals and plants.

Teleosaurus *tel ee oh SAWR us* A sea-living crocodile that lived in Jurassic times.

V W

vertebrates Animals that possess a backbone. They include fish, amphibians, reptiles, birds, and mammals.

warm-blooded Animals that are warm-blooded maintain a constant body temperature that is usually above that of the outside air. Birds and mammals are warm-blooded. *See* COLD-BLOODED.

Famous Dinosaur Localities Around the World

Argentina Finds of giant sauropods and armored dinosaurs of the Cretaceous age.

Bernissart, Belgium Remains of a number of Iguanodon specimens found in 1877 and 1878 are now displayed at the Natural History Museum in Brussels. In all there are 11 mounted skeletons and 20 others.

Crystal Palace, London A famous series of full-size dinosaur models were shown at the Great Exhibition of 1854. They were made by Benjamin Waterhouse Hawkins under the direction of Professor Richard Owen. The models can still be seen, although many of them are now known to be inaccurate.

Como Bluff, Wyoming A site worked by Professor Marsh's men particularly during the period 1877–1880. It yielded many skeletons, including a complete one of Stegosaurus.

Connecticut Valley, New England, U.S.A. The site of America's oldest dinosaur finds, and particularly noted for its fossil footprints.

Dinosaur National Monument, Utah A living museum in which Jurassic dinosaurs are still being extracted from the rock.

Gobi Desert and **Mongolia** This remote part of the world has been visited by a number of expeditions, and is famous for the many finds of fossils of Cretaceous dinosaurs. The fossils include nests of eggs of Protoceratops. In the early 1920's, the American Museum of Natural History sent an expedition to the area. More recently, Polish and Russian paleontologists have visited the sites.

Solnhofen, Bavaria, West Germany Not a dinosaur site, but the place where the first fossils of Archaeopteryx were discovered in 1861 and 1872.

Tendaguru, Tanzania A Jurassic site excavated by both German and British paleontologists during the first half of the 20th century. The many finds have included Brachiosaurus, animals related to Stegosaurus, and flying reptiles.

Creatures
Great & Small

What are the simplest animals?

THE SIMPLEST ANIMALS There are well over a million different kinds of animals. They vary greatly in almost every way—in shape, in color, in habits, and in intelligence. Some are timid, and some are ferocious. The blue whale may be more than 100 feet (30 meters) in length. But many simple, single-celled creatures are much too small to be seen with the unaided eye.

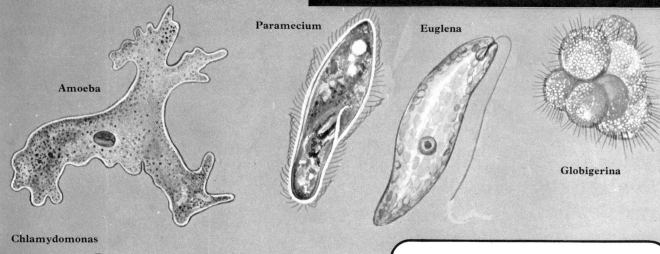

Paramecium

Euglena

Amoeba

Globigerina

Chlamydomonas

Noctiluca

Gonyaulax

The simplest animals, called *protozoans*, are extremely varied. Some are naked blobs of jelly, while others are covered with hundreds of tiny hairs, or have one or two long hair-like whips. Still others have beautiful, elaborate shells.

How do they move?

Each kind of single-celled animal moves in a distinctive way. Some animals beat their whip-like flagella. Amoeba pushes out fingers of jelly. Paramecium rows itself through the water by waving its tiny hairs called *cilia*.

Euglena moves sometimes with a squirming action.

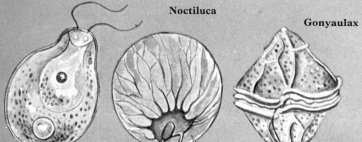

Amoeba moves by pushing out fingers of jelly, or pseudopodia.

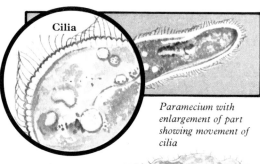

Cilia

Paramecium with enlargement of part showing movement of cilia

Stylonichia crawling

How do they eat?

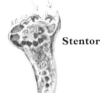

Didinium pierces a Paramecium.

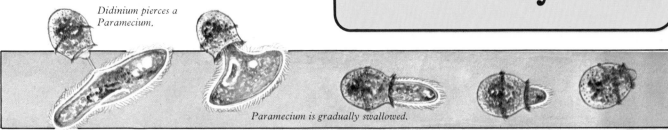

Paramecium is gradually swallowed.

Stentor

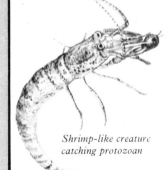

Amoeba eating another tiny protozoan

Didinium feeds by piercing and then swallowing its prey. Stentor draws tiny food particles into its gullet by beating its cilia. Amoeba flows around its food, engulfing it.

An Animal Puzzle

No one is quite sure which other animals are related to sponges. A sponge seems rather like a lot of single-celled animals joined together to form a colony. But scientists know that a sponge is really more complicated than this.

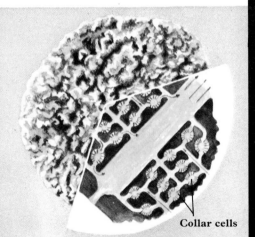

Collar cells

Slice of sponge wall highly magnified

Do they have any enemies?

Shrimp-like creature catching protozoan

Protozoans are eaten by numerous other small animals, including other protozoans. Tiny shrimp-like animals, worms of many kinds, wheel animals, and a host of other creatures prey on them. Often, these creatures create feeding currents that sweep the protozoans into their mouths.

Are they harmful?

Blood cells

Malaria parasite

Female mosquito sucking blood

Many protozoans are *parasites*, living inside—or on the outside of—other animals. In humans, perhaps the best known parasite is the one that causes malaria. This parasite is carried by female mosquitoes. When a mosquito feeds, by piercing a person's skin and sucking up blood, the malaria parasite enters the bloodstream.

What are the "flower animals" like?

FLOWERS OF THE SEA Some creatures look more like flowers than like animals. They include corals, sea anemones, jellyfish, and hydras. These animals are the coelenterates—the hollow-bodied animals. Although they are simple animals, their bodies are made up of many cells arranged in two layers around a cavity in which food is digested. They live in rivers, lakes, and the sea. Sometimes, groups of them form underwater "gardens" of great beauty, hidden away where only the fishes can normally see them.

Portuguese man-of-war

There are two main forms of flower animals. One is the hollow, tube-like polyp, such as Hydra, with a ring of tentacles around its mouth. The other is the often more bell-shaped medusa of the typical jellyfish. Sometimes the same animal has both polyps and medusae—just to make matters confusing!

Jellyfish

How do they move?

Some jellyfish are able to swim freely in the sea. Others drift in the surface currents. But Hydras can move along the bottom of ponds by somersaulting. They bend over and stand on their heads. Then they bend again to return to the upright position, using their tentacles.

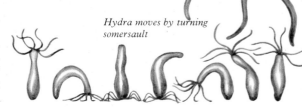

Hydra moves by turning somersault

Is coral alive?

If you watch coral carefully, hundreds of tiny hydra-like coral animals can be seen poking out from cup-shaped pits in the hard stony coral formation. Each has its tentacles out, ready to catch food.

How is a coral reef formed?

Coral is a hard "skeleton" produced by millions of tiny hydra-like animals. It is made mostly of carbonate of lime. The chalky skeletons build up year after year, forming reefs. There are three kinds of coral reefs.

Fringing reef forming around island

Barrier reef—formed from fringing reef as land sinks

Atoll formed when land has sunk below the sea surface, leaving coral reef surrounding lagoon

How do the "flower animals" catch their food?

All flower animals have stinging cells. These are used to stun food. Sea anemones can catch quite large animals such as fish in their tentacles. Other types feed by beating cilia to create a current of water. This current sweeps tiny plant and animal food particles into their mouths.

Sea anemones closed up

Sea anemone with fish trapped in tentacles

Are there many kinds of worms?

WORMS OF ALL KINDS Worms are soft-bodied animals that move by crawling. Flatworms, roundworms, leeches, ringed worms, tapeworms, bristle worms, hair worms—these are just some of the many creatures that are included in the various worm groups. Some live in the soil, others live in water, and some make their home on (or inside) plants or other animals. Sometimes, they cause diseases. Even human beings can be seriously affected by them.

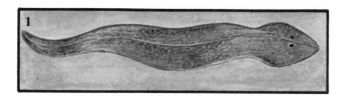

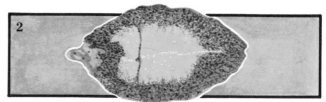

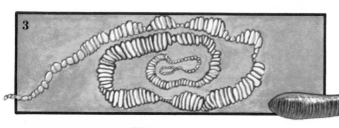

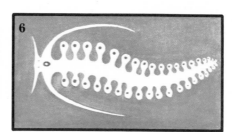

The many kinds of worms belong to several different groups of animals. They include flat-worms (1,2), tapeworm (3), earthworm (4), the tube-building peacock worm (5), Tomopteris, a bristle worm (6), leech (7), flat worm that feeds on sea-squirts (8), bristle worm (9), and fanworms (10).

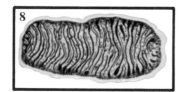

How do they move?

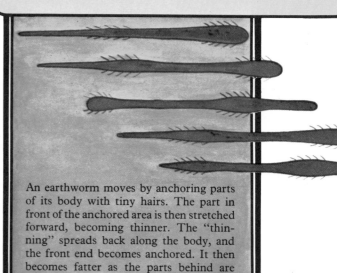

An earthworm moves by anchoring parts of its body with tiny hairs. The part in front of the anchored area is then stretched forward, becoming thinner. The "thinning" spreads back along the body, and the front end becomes anchored. It then becomes fatter as the parts behind are pulled forward.

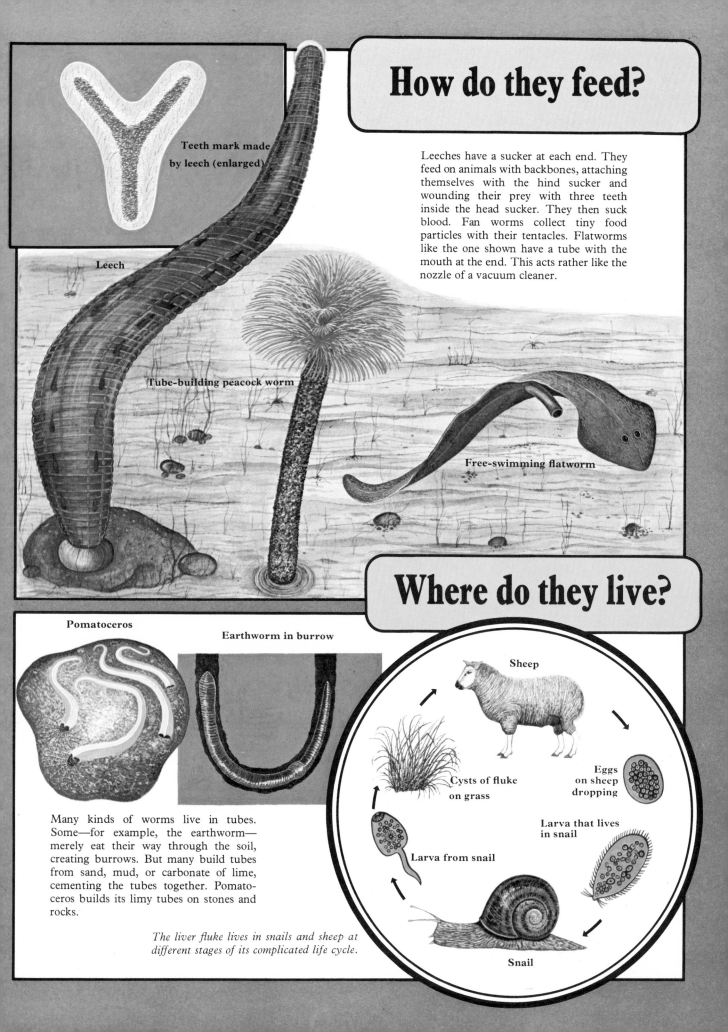

Teeth mark made by leech (enlarged)

Leech

Tube-building peacock worm

Free-swimming flatworm

How do they feed?

Leeches have a sucker at each end. They feed on animals with backbones, attaching themselves with the hind sucker and wounding their prey with three teeth inside the head sucker. They then suck blood. Fan worms collect tiny food particles with their tentacles. Flatworms like the one shown have a tube with the mouth at the end. This acts rather like the nozzle of a vacuum cleaner.

Where do they live?

Pomatoceros

Earthworm in burrow

Many kinds of worms live in tubes. Some—for example, the earthworm—merely eat their way through the soil, creating burrows. But many build tubes from sand, mud, or carbonate of lime, cementing the tubes together. Pomatoceros builds its limy tubes on stones and rocks.

The liver fluke lives in snails and sheep at different stages of its complicated life cycle.

Sheep

Cysts of fluke on grass

Eggs on sheep dropping

Larva that lives in snail

Larva from snail

Snail

Where do molluscs live?

Molluscs can be found almost anywhere—on land, in ponds and streams, and in the sea. They may burrow in sand, mud, wood or rock. Each type of mollusc has its own pattern of life. It is adapted for living in its particular surroundings.

LIFE IN A SHELL Anyone who has ever walked along a beach has picked up and admired shells of many different colors and of various shapes—some single, some double, some flat, and some spiral. The animals that live in (or once lived in) these shells are called molluscs. Their name comes from a Latin word meaning "soft-bodied." Not all molluscs have a shell, but each of them has a soft body and a muscular foot. They include snails, slugs, octopuses, and squids.

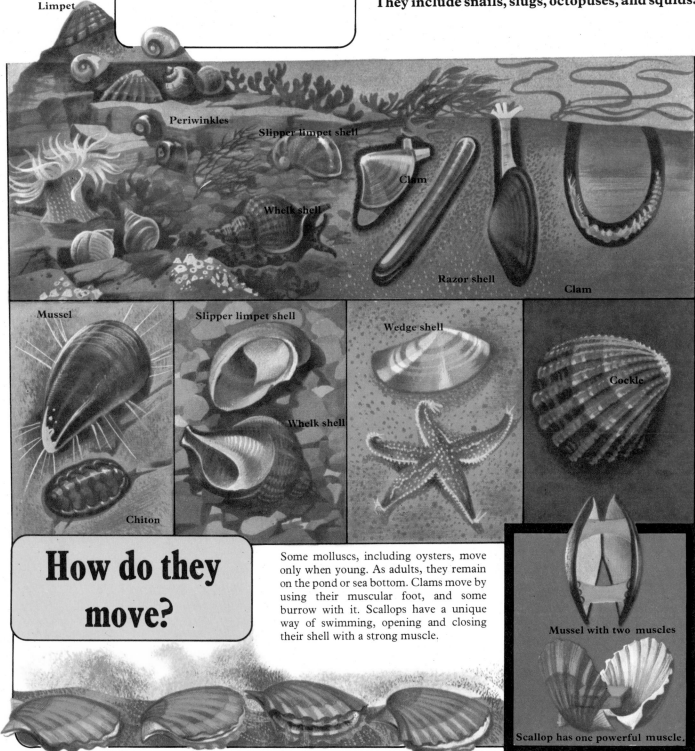

Limpet

Periwinkles

Slipper limpet shell

Clam

Whelk shell

Razor shell

Clam

Mussel

Slipper limpet shell

Wedge shell

Cockle

Whelk shell

Chiton

Mussel with two muscles

Scallop has one powerful muscle.

How do they move?

Some molluscs, including oysters, move only when young. As adults, they remain on the pond or sea bottom. Clams move by using their muscular foot, and some burrow with it. Scallops have a unique way of swimming, opening and closing their shell with a strong muscle.

What do they eat?

Cuttlefish catching its prey

Many molluscs feed on other animals. Cuttlefish have five pairs of tentacles, two larger than the others. These grasp such prey as prawns and shrimp by means of suckers. The prey is passed to other tentacles, and into the mouth, which has horny jaws.

Section through mollusc's stomach

Food out

Food in

Tellina with its tubes (siphons) pushed out. Water carrying food is drawn in though one toward the mouth. Waste flows out through the other.

Can they defend themselves against enemies?

The squid is a master of color change. Its skin has special pigment cells that can change size rapidly to vary the skin color. Squid are fast swimmers, and have an ink sac from which ink can be ejected into the water to confuse enemies.

What is a pearl?

Pearls are formed in the soft parts of such molluscs as oysters and mussels. They are made of *nacre* (mother of pearl). Pearls are built up by the tissues of the oyster around an invading body, such as a tapeworm or even a grain of sand. The "invader" is gradually enclosed in layers of mother of pearl, and in time the round gem is created.

Pearl

Are all starfish "five pointed"?

THE SPINY-SKINNED ANIMALS Starfish, brittle stars, sea urchins, sand dollars, sea lilies, and sea cucumbers are quite different from any other types of animals. They have a basic five-rayed body plan. All their parts are arranged around a central point, or along a central line. The outer layer of the bodies of these animals contains chalky plates and spines, and, as a result, they feel rough and spiky to the touch. All of them live in the sea, and they are found in most parts of the oceans.

Starfish

Although all starfish have a basic five-rayed body plan, not all of them take the characteristic "five-pointed" form of the common starfish (above).

Serpent star

Feather star

Sea cucumber

Can they re-grow arms that break off?

Starfish can re-grow all their arms if they break off. Because the mouth and digestive organs are in the central disk, a starfish without arms can still feed. New arms will grow eventually from the disk.

How do they feed?

Starfish have rows of tube feet on the undersides of their arms. Each foot is a small, hollow "finger" with a tiny sucker at the end. A single foot is not very strong. But a group of feet together can exert enough pull to open a mussel for the starfish to eat.

Starfish

Scallop

What do other spiny-skinned animals look like?

Most other spiny-skinned animals look very different from starfish. Sea urchins have a hard shell protecting their soft parts. Rows of tube feet poke through the shell, which is covered in spines and small pincers. Sea cucumbers look like giant pickles. Sea lilies live attached to the sea bed on long stalks.

Sea lily

Can sea urchins move?

Sea urchins are able to move their globe-like bodies by using their tiny tube feet. After each foot moves, it holds on to the rock surface with the tiny sucker at its tip. The sea urchin can either walk on its tube feet, or pull itself along up a slope. On level ground, the spines can be used as well.

Sea urchin

Purple sea urchin

Common sea urchin (empty shell)

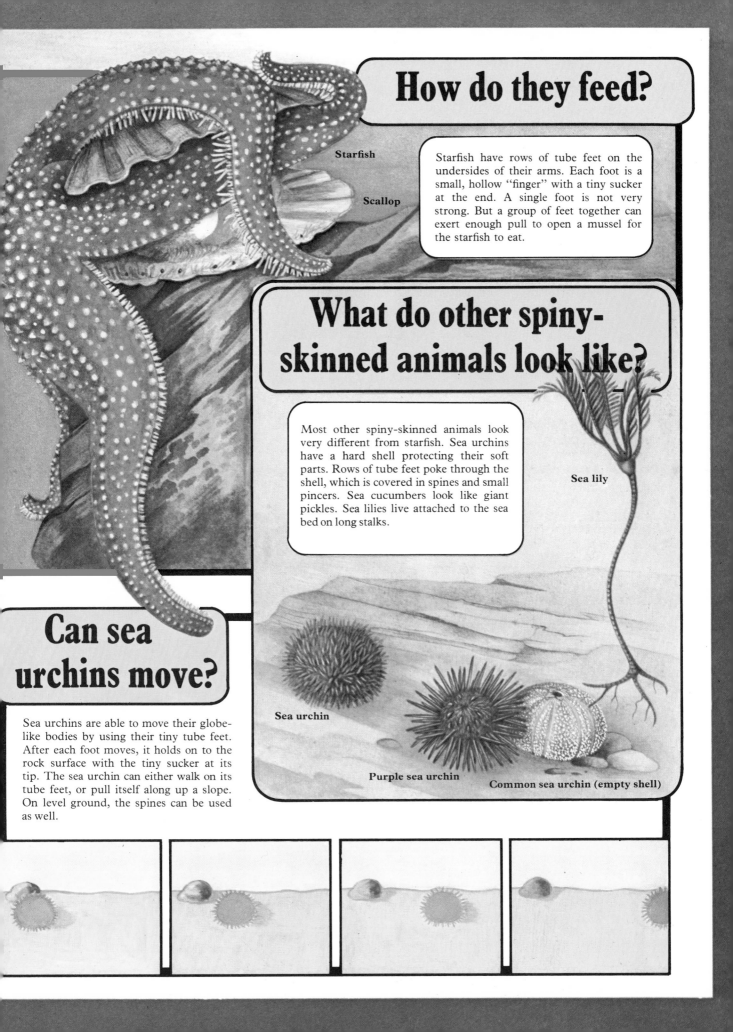

How does a crab differ from a lobster?

KNIGHTS IN ARMOR Thousands of different species of animals with flexible, jointed shells or crusts live on land or in the sea. They are known as crustacea. Probably, the best-known members of the crustacea are crabs, crayfish, shrimps, and prawns, but most crustaceans are much smaller than these animals. One numerous sea-living group are the oar-footed animals called copepods.

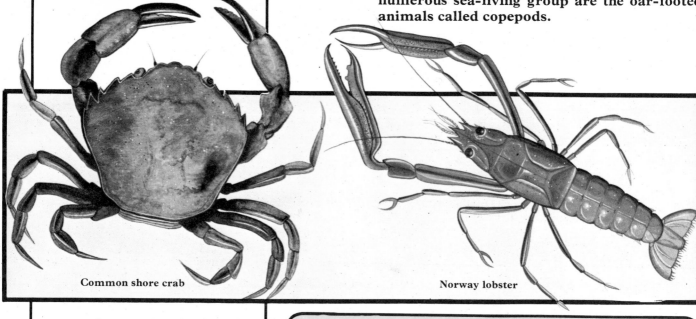

Common shore crab

Norway lobster

Crabs and lobsters are closely related animals. They have ten legs, arranged in five pairs on the underside of the chest region. But there are differences, as the pictures show. Crabs are flattened, and have tail segments that fold underneath their bodies. Lobsters have a tail fan. The larvae differ too.

How do crustaceans feed?

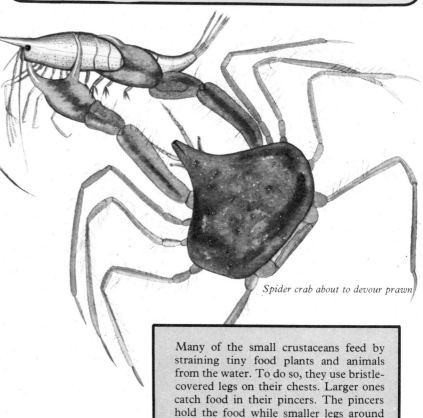

Spider crab about to devour prawn

Do any of them live on land?

Woodlice are the only crustaceans fully adapted for life on land—though some crabs, shore slaters, and others spend a lot of time out of water. Also called *pill bugs* and *sow bugs*, woodlice have to live in damp surroundings.

Many of the small crustaceans feed by straining tiny food plants and animals from the water. To do so, they use bristle-covered legs on their chests. Larger ones catch food in their pincers. The pincers hold the food while smaller legs around the mouth chew it ready for swallowing.

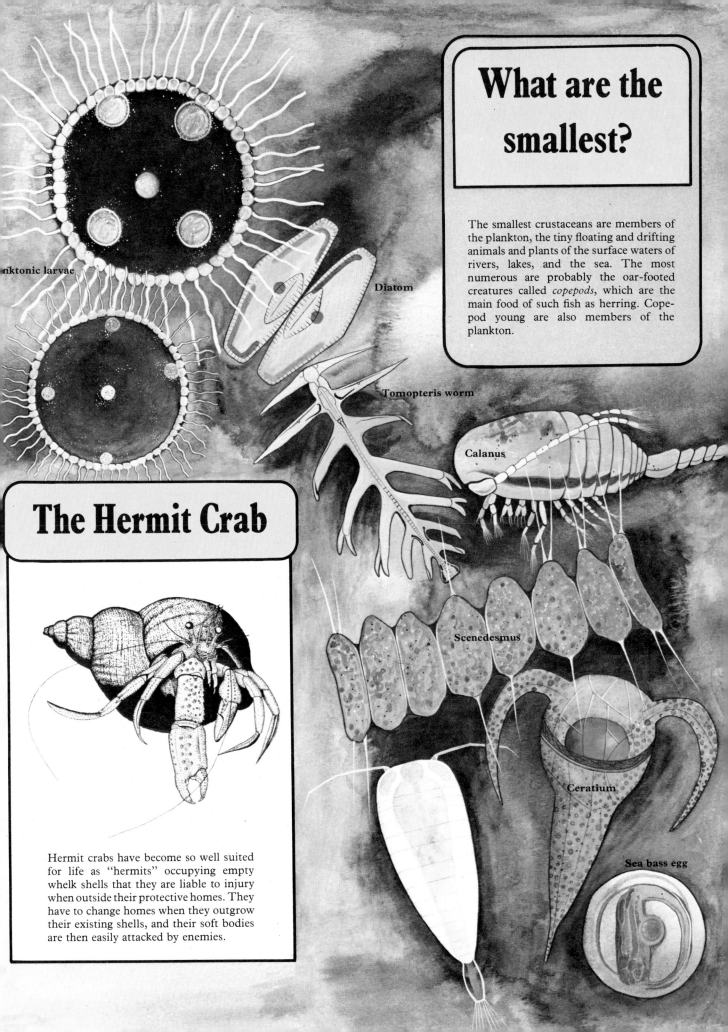

nktonic larvae

Diatom

What are the smallest?

The smallest crustaceans are members of the plankton, the tiny floating and drifting animals and plants of the surface waters of rivers, lakes, and the sea. The most numerous are probably the oar-footed creatures called *copepods*, which are the main food of such fish as herring. Copepod young are also members of the plankton.

Tomopteris worm

Calanus

The Hermit Crab

Scenedesmus

Ceratium

Sea bass egg

Hermit crabs have become so well suited for life as "hermits" occupying empty whelk shells that they are liable to injury when outside their protective homes. They have to change homes when they outgrow their existing shells, and their soft bodies are then easily attacked by enemies.

Is a spider an insect?

THE WORLD OF INSECTS Insects resemble the crustacea in having a hard, protective outer shell that is jointed like a suit of armor. They are distinctive in having a body that is divided into three parts—head, thorax, and abdomen. They have a system of breathing tubes. All adult insects have six legs. Most of them have wings attached to the thorax, and these are often brightly colored. Insects are by far the largest group of animals. They live on land and in fresh water.

If you look carefully at a spider, you will see that it has eight legs and only two main parts to its body. An insect has six legs and a three-part body. The hind part of a spider's body is not made up of sections as an insect's is. And a spider's eyes are always single units, not several.

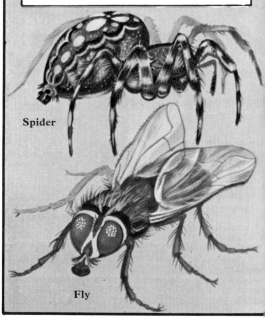

Spider

Fly

What is a caterpillar?

A caterpillar hatches from an egg. It feeds and grows much larger, shedding its skin several times, and then changes into a *chrysalis* or *pupa*. Often, it will spend winter in this form before emerging as a butterfly. Many other insects have similar life histories. *Right*, the changes in a cabbage white butterfly's life cycle, from the time the female adult butterfly lays her eggs on a cabbage leaf until a new adult emerges.

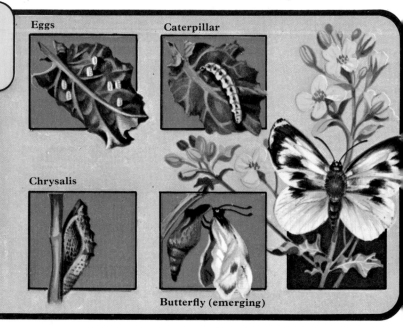

Eggs

Caterpillar

Chrysalis

Butterfly (emerging)

Butterfly feeding from flower

Dragonfly catching its prey on the wing

How do insects feed?

Greenfly

Mosquito

Insects feed on plants and animals, and many are pests. Their mouthparts vary according to the way they feed. Mosquitoes have piercing and sucking mouths. Butterflies and moths have long tubes for sucking nectar from flowers. And dragonflies have powerful biting mouthparts, as do many ants and wasps.

Do they live in groups?

Insects that live in groups or colonies are called *social insects*. Examples are bees, wasps, ants, and termites. Each group has members of various kinds. For instance, termites may be workers or soldiers. Or their function may be to breed. Among breeding termites are the king and queen, who form the colony.

Combs of the honey bee. Eggs can be seen in some of the cells.

Section through a wood ants' nest showing the different types of individual. The queen ant is the large ant near the center of the nest.

Can they talk to each other?

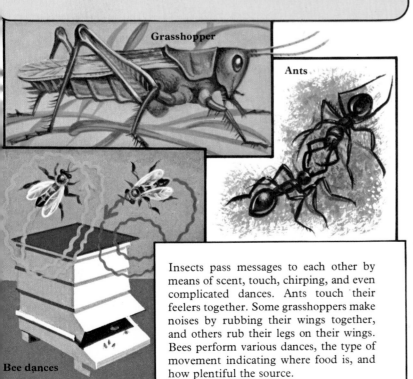
Grasshopper

Ants

Bee dances

Insects pass messages to each other by means of scent, touch, chirping, and even complicated dances. Ants touch their feelers together. Some grasshoppers make noises by rubbing their wings together, and others rub their legs on their wings. Bees perform various dances, the type of movement indicating where food is, and how plentiful the source.

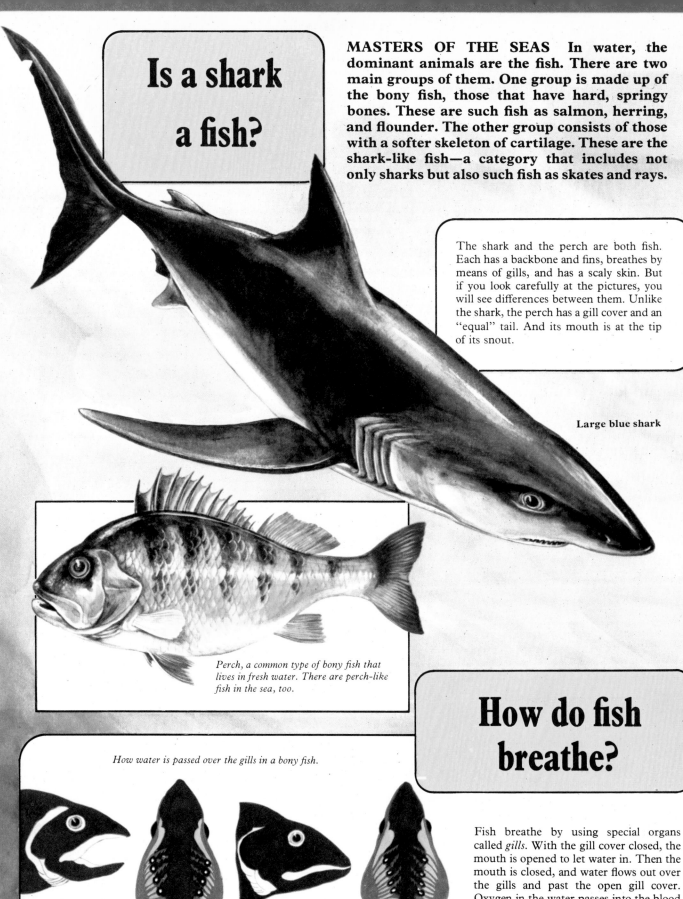

Is a shark a fish?

MASTERS OF THE SEAS In water, the dominant animals are the fish. There are two main groups of them. One group is made up of the bony fish, those that have hard, springy bones. These are such fish as salmon, herring, and flounder. The other group consists of those with a softer skeleton of cartilage. These are the shark-like fish—a category that includes not only sharks but also such fish as skates and rays.

The shark and the perch are both fish. Each has a backbone and fins, breathes by means of gills, and has a scaly skin. But if you look carefully at the pictures, you will see differences between them. Unlike the shark, the perch has a gill cover and an "equal" tail. And its mouth is at the tip of its snout.

Large blue shark

Perch, a common type of bony fish that lives in fresh water. There are perch-like fish in the sea, too.

How do fish breathe?

How water is passed over the gills in a bony fish.

Mouth open   **Gill cover closed**   **Mouth closed**   **Gill cover open**

Fish breathe by using special organs called *gills*. With the gill cover closed, the mouth is opened to let water in. Then the mouth is closed, and water flows out over the gills and past the open gill cover. Oxygen in the water passes into the blood supply in the gill tissues, and waste carbon dioxide is washed away into the water.

Can any fish live out of water?

Several kinds of fish spend long periods on land, or can cope with dry conditions. Lungfish breathe air, and those that live in Africa and South America can survive for long periods when the rivers dry up. The climbing perch of India lives mostly on land. Mudskippers are even able to walk, using their fins as legs.

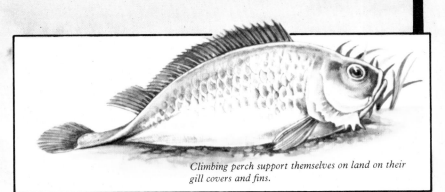

Mudskippers are able to spend much of the time out of water. Some species even climb trees.

African lungfish lives through dry season by burrowing into mud of river bed and surrounding itself with mucus. It can survive until the river reappears.

Climbing perch support themselves on land on their gill covers and fins.

How do they look after their young?

Many fish just lay their eggs and leave them to grow. Sometimes, one or both parents look after them. The stickleback builds a complicated nest, and the bitterling lays its eggs inside a swan mussel. Such lake fish as the Tilapia protect their young in their mouths when danger threatens.

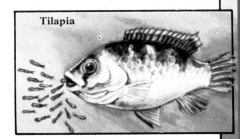

Sticklebacks with their nest

Tilapia

Do they travel far?

Salmon and some trout travel long distances up rivers from the sea to breed. Eels swim thousands of miles from the rivers of Europe and the eastern USA to spawn in the Sargasso Sea, in the Caribbean.

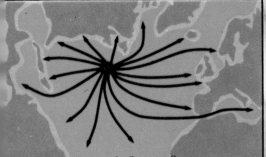

Eels migrate to the Sargasso Sea to breed.

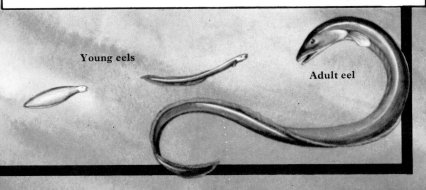

Young eels

Adult eel

Why do amphibians live on land and in water?

TWO WAYS OF LIFE The animals of o[ne] large group are amphibians—that is, they spe[nd] part of their life in water and part on lan[d]. Among the most common amphibians are fro[gs], toads, newts, and salamanders. Amphibians a[re] cold-blooded animals, whose temperature vari[es] according to their surroundings. General[ly] they have a moist skin and live in damp place[s]. They vary considerably. For example, adu[lt] frogs and toads are tailless, but newts have tai[ls].

Most amphibians have to return to water each year to breed. Frogs and newts, for example, lay their eggs in water—either singly or in masses that form the familiar frog spawn. The young, called *tadpoles*, hatch out as fish-like creatures, and live in water. They feed on water plants, and slowly change into adults.

Adult frog

Stages in a frog's development : from egg to adult takes about 6 weeks.

Front legs appear a few weeks later

Hind legs appear at about six weeks

Rapidly growing tadpole (outside gills disappear)

Growing tadpole with feathery gills

Eggs

Young tadpole

How does a frog catch its food?

Adult frogs feed mainly on insects, but also eat worms, slugs, snails, spiders, and other small animals. A frog's tongue is attached to the floor of its mouth, and can be flicked out some distance by powerful muscles. Its tip is covered with a sticky substance.

How does it move?

Frogs are able to move rapidly on land and in water. The muscles of the hind legs are arranged so that the bent legs can be straightened suddenly, enabling the frog to jump or swim quickly. The short, stocky front legs act as shock absorbers in landing.

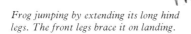

Frog jumping by extending its long hind legs. The front legs brace it on landing.

Frog swimming

Do amphibians have tails?

Crested newt

Mud salamander

Axolotl

Mud puppy

Frogs and toads, the best known amphibians, only have tails as tadpoles. But many other amphibians have tails as adults. Examples are newts, salamanders, and strange creatures with no legs called *apodans*. One giant salamander is nearly as long as an adult human being.

Midwife Toad

Male midwife toad carrying strings of eggs wrapped between its hind legs. The tadpoles develop there within the eggs for about three weeks, and the male toad then places the eggs into water where they quickly finish their development and hatch into tadpoles.

The midwife toad gets its name from the male's strange habit of carrying the eggs before these are laid in water.

How many kinds of reptiles are there?

THE REPTILES Reptiles are cold-blooded animals, but are completely equipped for life on land. They have lungs and breathe air from the atmosphere. Their skins are scaly. Most of them lay eggs similar to birds' eggs. The shells keep the eggs from drying out. Some of the commonest reptiles are lizards, snakes, crocodiles, alligators, and tortoises. In the past, in the age of the great reptiles called dinosaurs, they were the dominant animals on Earth.

Only four main groups of reptiles survive from the days, millions of years ago, when the great reptiles called dinosaurs ruled the world. These are the snakes and lizards, the crocodiles, the tortoises and turtles, and the New Zealand tuatara, which forms a group on its own. Snakes and lizards are the most numerous.

Where do they live?

Turtle

Turtle egg hatching

Amphibians still show their evolution from fish-like creatures by returning to water to breed. But reptiles are fully fitted to live on land. Even the turtles, which live in water, have to return to land to breed. They lay their eggs in holes dug in the sand. After hatching, the young go back to the sea.

How does a snake eat?

Python

Pythons and some other snakes kill their prey by crushing. Vipers and most others kill by injecting poison. A viper's skull is so constructed that a poison fang is pushed into the prey as the jaws close. Because a snake's top and bottom jaws are joined only by an elastic ligament, prey larger than the snake can be swallowed.

Snake skull

Fang

Lower jaw

Why does a snake flick its tongue in and out?

When a snake flicks out its tongue, it is not threatening a victim, but merely sampling the air around it. Tiny fragments of chemicals in the air stick to the tongue, and are tested by a special organ in the roof of the snake's mouth.

Can lizards really change their color?

Chameleon

Lizards have striking color patterns, and many kinds are able to change color. Chameleons have earned a reputation as masters of disguise as they stalk their prey.

Why do birds have feathers?

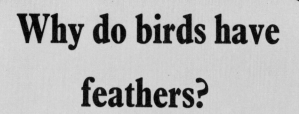

RULERS OF THE AIR Birds are probably the commonest, the best loved, and—often—the most beautiful of wild animals. Like reptiles, they have scales, but only on their legs. They also resemble reptiles in laying eggs that have shells. But they are unique in having feathers. Their feathered wings give them a freedom of movement that few other creatures in the animal kingdom can match.

Swallow

Young pheasant

Peacock

Tufted duck

Vane

Quill feather   Shaft

Enlargement of part of quill feather

Down feather (such feathers help to keep young birds warm)

The feathers of birds serve a variety of purposes. They provide a warm, protective covering, helping to keep the bird warm. They also play an important part in flying. Their color helps both to conceal the bird from its enemies and to attract a mate at breeding times.

How does a bird fly?

Albatross

Flamingo

Birds fly by flapping their wings, and by gliding and soaring on air currents. To fly, a bird must have a large surface area compared to its volume. This is why most birds have small bodies. But the wings are comparatively large, and provide the large surface area necessary. In flapping flight, the wings are moved, not straight up and down, but downwards and forwards and then backwards and upwards. This creates a flow of air over the top surface of the wings that lifts the bird upwards and propels it forward. Soaring birds, such as buzzards, have broad wings, and use rising warm air currents. Gliding birds, such as seagulls, use the fast-flowing air currents near cliffs and at the water surface.

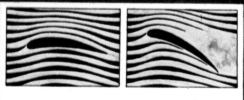

Flow of air over wing shape. Tilting the wing (right) drags the wing down. The air flow over the upper surface (left) lifts the wing upwards.

Pigeon

How do birds build their nests?

Adélie penguin has a simple nest of stones.

Some birds, including the Emperor penguin, do not build nests at all. Adélie penguins have bare stone nests. But many birds construct complicated "nurseries" for their young. Mud, moss, lichens, twigs, straw, hair, and feathers may all be used as building materials.

Australian brush turkey (below) hatches eggs, using the heat produced in a mound of rotting leaves and other vegetation.

Green woodpecker (above) drills a hole in a tree trunk.

Some perching birds line their nests with all sorts of materials, such as grass, feathers, and moss.

Are there many fierce birds?

Eagle

Owl

Secretary bird

Birds of prey have hooked beaks and sharp, curved claws for catching and holding their prey while feeding. Some, such as vultures, feed mostly on dead animals, tearing the flesh off with their beaks.

Why do some birds migrate?

Many birds migrate over long distances. They take advantage of the better weather conditions and more plentiful supply of food available for breeding in northerly areas during the summer months.

What are the main kinds of mammals?

THE MAMMALS The most advanced of all animals are the mammals, the group of animals that includes horses, dogs, cats, rabbits, elephants, tigers, and whales. Humans, too, are mammals. All mammals feed their young on milk produced by their mammary (milk-giving) glands. Generally, young mammals develop within their mothers' bodies. But some mammals lay eggs.

Horse—a placental

Monkey

Koala—a pouched mammal

Elephant

Duck-billed platypus—lays eggs

Whale—the world's largest mammal

Bat—the only mammal that can fly

There are three main groups of mammals —those that lay eggs, such as the duck-billed platypus; those with pouches in which their young grow, such as the kangaroo; and the placental mammals, which give birth to more advanced young. Most are placentals.

How do they take care of their young?

Mammals spend a lot of time and energy looking after their young. The young are suckled on milk produced by the mother. They are often carried, groomed, and protected by the adults. This is particularly true of animals that live in herds, and of monkeys and apes, which form strong family groups.

Fox with cubs

Rhinoceros

What kind of homes do they live in?

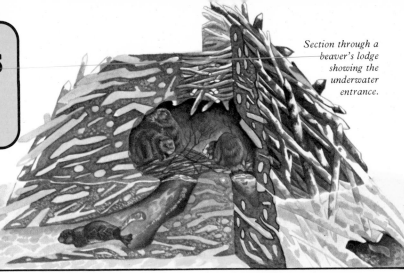

Section through a beaver's lodge showing the underwater entrance.

Many mammals construct nests. Rabbits, badgers, and many rodents burrow underground. Perhaps the master builders are beavers. They are able to fell trees by gnawing, and use them to dam streams and rivers, creating lakes in which to build their lodges.

European badgers have a large den underground called a "set." The nesting chamber is lined with moss and dried grass.

What do they eat?

Some mammals eat plants, others are meat eaters, or scavengers that eat almost anything. Cats and dogs have sharp teeth for piercing and tearing through flesh. Plant eaters have flat teeth for grinding. Rodents have chisel-like front teeth for gnawing.

Why do many of them live in herds?

On the great plains of Africa, vast herds of grazing animals can still be seen. They include zebra, wildebeest, and many kinds of antelopes and gazelles. By living together in large herds, these animals gain protection from their enemies, the big cats—lions, leopards, and cheetahs.

How many kinds of animals are there?

ANIMAL FACTS The variety of animals is almost endless. No human being has seen—or ever could see—all the different types of animals that exist. The insects alone consist of some 800,000 different kinds. And the individual members of each kind vary greatly among themselves. Some animals can move at amazing speed. Others seem reluctant to move at all unless they have to.

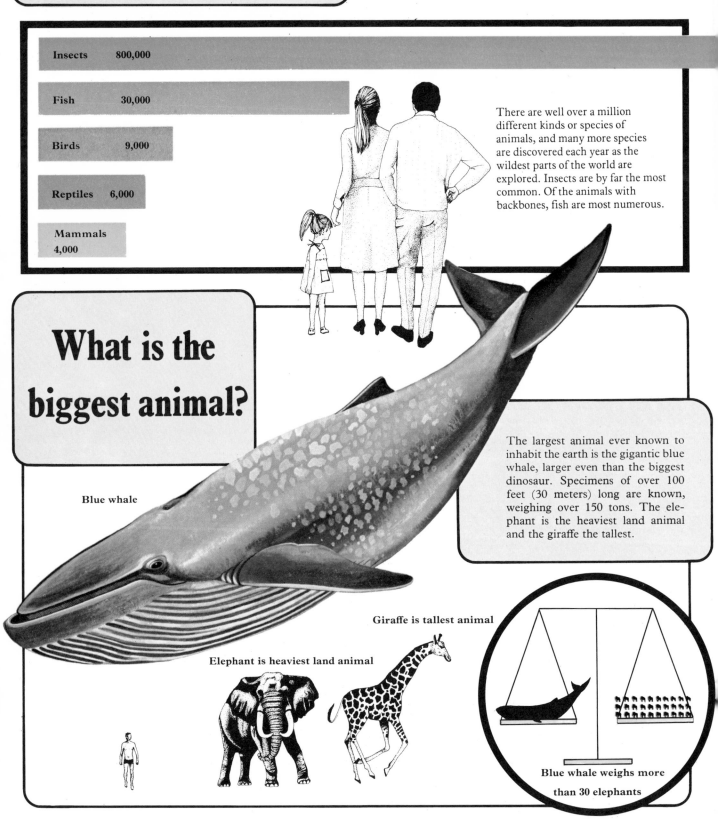

Insects	800,000
Fish	30,000
Birds	9,000
Reptiles	6,000
Mammals	4,000

There are well over a million different kinds or species of animals, and many more species are discovered each year as the wildest parts of the world are explored. Insects are by far the most common. Of the animals with backbones, fish are most numerous.

What is the biggest animal?

Blue whale

The largest animal ever known to inhabit the earth is the gigantic blue whale, larger even than the biggest dinosaur. Specimens of over 100 feet (30 meters) long are known, weighing over 150 tons. The elephant is the heaviest land animal and the giraffe the tallest.

Giraffe is tallest animal

Elephant is heaviest land animal

Blue whale weighs more than 30 elephants

What is the fastest?

The fastest creature ever recorded is the spine-tailed swift at 106 mph (170 kph). The cheetah is the fastest land animal.

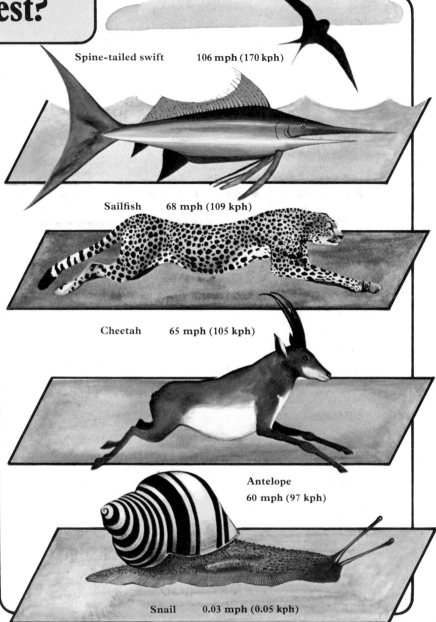

Spine-tailed swift   106 mph (170 kph)

Sailfish   68 mph (109 kph)

Cheetah   65 mph (105 kph)

Antelope
60 mph (97 kph)

Snail   0.03 mph (0.05 kph)

Which lives the longest?

Tortoise

The longest-lived animal is the tortoise — the oldest recorded age being over 152 years. Human beings have one of the longest life-spans, with 113 years being the oldest age recorded with any certainty.

Which is the greatest traveler?

Many animals migrate over long distances. Eels swim several thousand miles to breed, but birds are the champion travelers. Albatrosses wander many thousands of miles over the southern oceans, and the Arctic tern flies over 12,000 miles (19,000 km) each way from north to south and back on its annual migrations.

Arctic tern

Animal Defenses

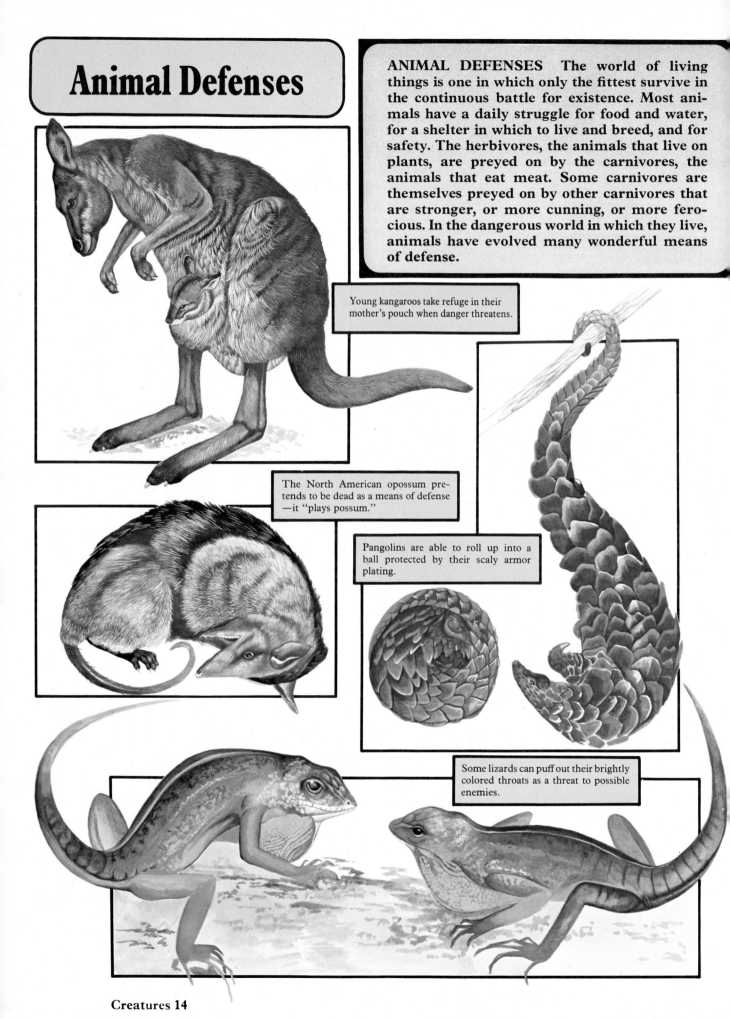

ANIMAL DEFENSES The world of living things is one in which only the fittest survive in the continuous battle for existence. Most animals have a daily struggle for food and water, for a shelter in which to live and breed, and for safety. The herbivores, the animals that live on plants, are preyed on by the carnivores, the animals that eat meat. Some carnivores are themselves preyed on by other carnivores that are stronger, or more cunning, or more ferocious. In the dangerous world in which they live, animals have evolved many wonderful means of defense.

Young kangaroos take refuge in their mother's pouch when danger threatens.

The North American opossum pretends to be dead as a means of defense —it "plays possum."

Pangolins are able to roll up into a ball protected by their scaly armor plating.

Some lizards can puff out their brightly colored throats as a threat to possible enemies.

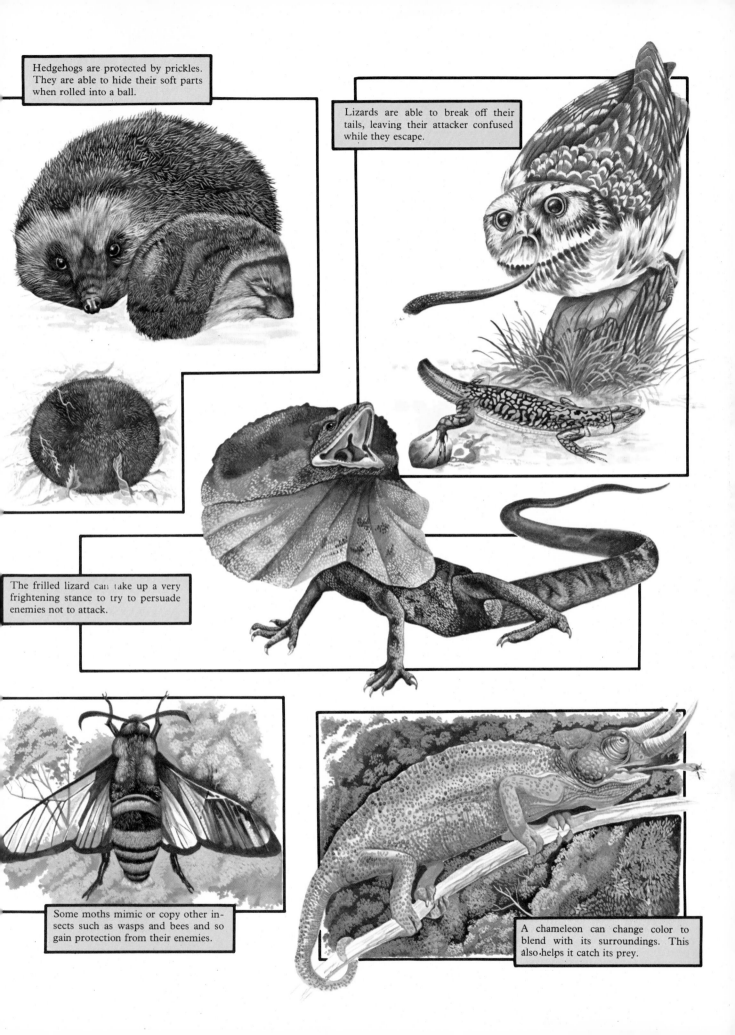

Hedgehogs are protected by prickles. They are able to hide their soft parts when rolled into a ball.

Lizards are able to break off their tails, leaving their attacker confused while they escape.

The frilled lizard can take up a very frightening stance to try to persuade enemies not to attack.

Some moths mimic or copy other insects such as wasps and bees and so gain protection from their enemies.

A chameleon can change color to blend with its surroundings. This also helps it catch its prey.

A-Z of Animal Life

A

abdomen In mammals, the part of the body that contains the stomach, intestines, kidney, liver, and reproductive organs. In insects and other arthropods, it is the hind section of the body. *See* INSECTS; MAMMALS.

amphibians The group of backboned animals that are capable of living both in water and on land, such as frogs, toads, newts, and salamanders. They are cold-blooded. Amphibians must return to the water to breed.

antennae The feelers on the head of various arthropods. *See* ARTHROPODS.

anthropoid Like the human form.

antlers The outgrowths on the head of male deer that, unlike true horns, are grown and shed yearly.

arboreal Living in trees.

arthropods The group of animals that includes insects, spiders, scorpions, crustaceans, centipedes, and millipedes. It is the largest division of the animal kingdom, containing about 80 per cent of all animal species. The body of an arthropod is made up of a row of similar parts, called segments. It has no backbone.

B

benthos The animals and plants that live on the sea or lake floor. For example, corals and sponges.

binomial system The method of naming animals in which each type of animal is given two Latin names. The first is the generic name (genus). It always begins with a capital letter. The second is the specific name (species). For example, the domestic dog is called *Canis familiaris*; that is, the domestic dog is a species of the genus *Canis*. *See* CLASSIFICATION; GENUS; LINNAEUS, CAROLUS; SPECIES.

bivalves The molluscs whose shells have two parts, usually hinged together. The most common examples are the edible molluscs, such as clams, mussels, oysters, and scallops. *See* MOLLUSCS.

C

carnivores The group of mainly flesh-eating mammals. The word is also used to mean *any* flesh-eating animals.

carrion Dead and rotting flesh which is eaten by scavengers, such as vultures.

cell The basic structural unit from which all living things are built. A cell may be a complete living package, capable of feeding, growing, and often of reproducing and even moving independently. In many-celled animals, there are several different types of cell, each of which has a particular job to do—for example, blood cells, bone cells, and nerve cells.

chrysalis The resting or pupa stage of a developing butterfly or moth, which occurs between its larva or caterpillar stage and its adult form. *See* LARVA; METAMORPHOSIS; PUPA.

classification The sorting or division of the animal and plant kingdoms into groups of animals with common characteristics. These groups range from the simple major divisions to the more detailed, and are arranged in an order to form a kind of family tree, as follows: phylum, class, order, family, genus, species. *See* BINOMIAL SYSTEM; GENUS; SPECIES.

coelenterates The group of animals that have a hollow body made of two layers of cells. They are the simplest animals that have nerve cells. Hydra, sea anemones, jellyfishes, and corals are coelenterates.

cold-blooded Animals whose body temperature changes with the temperature of their surroundings are said to be *cold-blooded*. The cold-blooded animals are fishes, amphibians, reptiles, and all the invertebrates. *See* WARM-BLOODED.

crustaceans The group of arthropods that includes lobsters, crabs, shrimps, crayfish, waterfleas, barnacles, and woodlice. The majority of the 36,000 known species live in water. Woodlice are land crustaceans. Crustaceans have two pairs of antennae and breathe, like fish, through gills. *See* ARTHROPODS.

D

Darwin, Charles Robert (1809–82) English naturalist who put forward the theory of evolution based on natural selection in his book *The Origin of the Species*. *See* EVOLUTION.

digestion The process by which the food eaten by an animal is broken down into chemicals that are easily absorbed by the animal. *See* RESPIRATION.

E

ecdysis The shedding of the hard outer casing or cuticle in young arthropods to allow for growth. A new larger cuticle forms.

ecology The study of communities of animals and plants and the ways in which they depend on one another and react to changes in their environments.

embryo An unborn animal in the process of development from the fertilized egg. It may be, for example, a chick inside its shell, or a young mammal inside its mother's womb. *See* FETUS.

evolution The process by which living things have developed from earlier simpler forms, and have become adapted to their environments. Evolution involves gradual change over very long periods of time, in some cases many millions of years. The idea was first put forward as a scientific proposition by Charles Darwin and Alfred Wallace.

F

fauna The animals of a particular region or of a certain geological period.

fertilization The joining of a male sex cell (*sperm*) to a female sex cell (*egg* or *ovum*) to produce a new individual.

fetus The embryo of a mammal in which all the main features, such as limbs, are recognizable. *See* EMBRYO.

food chain Flesh-eating animals eat other animals, which themselves feed either on other animals or on plants. But sooner or later, this process ends with plant-eating animals and plants. These food relationships in animal communities are called *food chains*.

fossil The preserved remains of an animal or plant that existed long ago. Most fossils are found in rocks, and are themselves filled with minerals which make them hard and stony. The age of a fossil is estimated from the layer of rock in which it is found. Fossils provide valuable information about early forms of life. *See* GEOLOGICAL PERIODS.

G

gasteropods The molluscs which have a flat sticky "foot" supporting the rest of the body. Gasteropods include snails, limpets, whelks, periwinkles, and slugs. Gasteropods are found on land and in water. *See* MOLLUSCS.

genus A group of closely related species of animals, all of which are given the same generic (group) name. *See* BINOMIAL SYSTEM; SPECIES.

geological periods The history of the Earth from its formation is divided into a number of periods based on the dates (in years before the present) at which major changes in the Earth's structure occurred.

H

habitat The place or environment in which an animal lives.

herbivore Any animal that feeds on plants.

heredity The way in which physical and mental characteristics are passed from parents to their offspring. *See* MENDEL, GREGOR.

hermaphrodite An animal which has both male and female reproductive organs in itself but cannot fertilize its own eggs. Earthworms are hermaphrodites.

hibernation The way some animals survive the winter conditions of extreme cold and food shortages by hiding away in specially prepared shelters. They fall into a very deep sleep, which lasts through the winter.

hybrid An animal resulting from the mating of two different species. Normally, a hybrid is unable to reproduce. A mule is the hybrid produced by the mating of a horse with a donkey.

I

imago The final or adult stage of an insect. *See* METAMORPHOSIS.

insectivores The group of small mammals that feed on insects, spiders, worms, and other small invertebrates. Moles, hedgehogs, and shrews are the main insectivores. The smallest living mammal is the Etruscan pygmy shrew, 2 to 3 inches (5 to 8 cm) long, including its tail.

insects These belong to the group of animals called *arthropods*. The body of an insect has three main parts: head, thorax, and abdomen. Most insects have three pairs of legs and one pair of antennae. Many have either one or two pairs of wings. Most insects live on land. All insects develop by the process called metamorphosis. There are over 800,000 named species of insects, which is about three-quarters of all animal species. Beetles form the largest group of insects with over 300,000 described species. *See* ARTHROPODS; METAMORPHOSIS.

instincts The forms of behavior that are born in an animal. Instinct tells an animal how to act in a particular situation without any necessity for learning what to do.

invertebrates All animals without backbones. The majority of animals are invertebrates. Examples are worms, insects, spiders, and octopuses. *See* VERTEBRATES.

L

larva The early form of an animal which has hatched from an egg and is quite unlike the adult. Certain insects, for example, lay eggs that hatch into larvae. The tadpole is the larval form of amphibians, such as the frog, toad, and newt. *See* METAMORPHOSIS; NYMPH.

Linnaeus, Carolus (1707–78) Swedish botanist who introduced the system of naming different types of plant and animal with two Latin terms, so that each can be clearly identified. *See* BINOMIAL SYSTEM; GENUS; SPECIES.

Lyell, Charles (1797–1875) Scottish geologist who first explained, in his book *Principles of Geology*, that rocks are arranged in layers (*strata*), and that the bottom layers are the oldest. *See* GEOLOGICAL PERIODS.

M

mammals The group of backboned animals whose young suckle on milk produced by their mothers. In most types of mammal, the young are born alive from inside the mother. But the most primitive mammals, duck-billed platypus and spiny anteater, lay shelled eggs. Mammals are warm-blooded and most species have a covering of hair. Most mammals live on the land, but some, such as whales and seals, live in the sea. Bats are the only mammals that can fly. The largest of all animals is the blue whale, over 100 feet (30 meters) in length and weighing over 100 tons. *See* INSECTIVORES; PRIMATES; UNGULATES.

marsupials The group of mammals whose females have pouches on their abdomens. They include the kangaroo, wallaby, wombat, and koala. A marsupial is born at an early stage in its development, and crawls unaided into its mother's pouch. There, it completes its development, attached to a nipple through which it gets milk.

Mendel, Gregor Johann (1822–84) Austrian monk and scientist who showed, mainly through his experiments on garden peas, how characteristics are passed from one generation to another.

metamorphosis The series of changes by which a larval form of an animal becomes an adult. Insects and amphibians undergo metamorphosis—for example, the change from caterpillar to butterfly or moth, and the change from tadpole to frog. *See* CHRYSALIS; IMAGO; LARVA; NYMPH; PUPA.

migration The regular and instinctive movement of animals from one place to another. Usually, the animals are moving between their summer and winter homes, or to and from their breeding grounds. Examples are swallows moving north in summer, and fishes swimming to spawning grounds.

mimicry The likeness of one species of animal to another species, or to some other object, so that protection or some other benefit is gained. The mimics may copy shape, color, or distinctive markings of the model (the original animal or object). The likeness is improved over many generations by natural selection. For example, a drone fly, which is harmless, mimics a bee to get protection. *See* WARNING COLORATION.

molluscs The group of animals that have a soft body without segments. They also have no backbone. The body is surrounded with a fold of skin, called the *mantle*. Many molluscs are protected by a shell. Molluscs include slugs and snails, clams, mussels, and oysters, squids, and octopuses. *See* BIVALVES; GASTEROPODS.

N

natural selection Darwin's theory that the animals best suited to an environment are more likely to survive and to reproduce. That is, there is "survival of the fittest." Over a long period of time, the conditions in an environment change, and the animals in that environment also change as they adapt to the new conditions. From this gradual process of change, new species of animals develop from the old. *See* DARWIN, CHARLES; EVOLUTION.

nekton Water animals that swim freely, as opposed to bottom-living benthos and floating plankton. *See* BENTHOS; PLANKTON.

nymph With certain insects, such as the dragonfly, the egg hatches out into a nymph that resembles the adult. *See* METAMORPHOSIS.

O

organ A part of an animal's body made up of various tissues that work together to do a particular job.

organism A living thing capable of growth and reproduction.

P

parasite An organism that lives on or inside another organism, which is called the *host*. The parasite takes food from the host but gives nothing in return. The host is not necessarily killed by the parasite.

placenta The specially formed organ in the womb of a mammal that enables oxygen, food, and waste products to pass between the embryo and the mother. The placenta is expelled after the birth of the baby animal.

plankton The tiny animals and plants that live and float freely near the surface of natural waters. It is the basic source of food in water life.

predator An animal that hunts, kills, and eats other animals.

primates The group of mammals that includes apes and monkeys, and also a few smaller animals, such as bushbabies, lemurs, and lorises. Humans, too, are primates. Primates' hands and feet can grasp. Many primates live in trees. Some monkeys have a gripping (prehensile) tail, which they use as a fifth limb when climbing or performing acrobatics. Anthropoid (human-like) apes, such as chimpanzees and gorillas, are different from monkeys because they have a more highly developed brain, long arms, and no tail. Gorillas are the largest living primates.

protoplasm The living material in cells. It is a complicated mixture of substances in which chemical changes are continuously taking place as a cell works. *See* CELL.

protozoans The group of organisms that are single-celled, such as amoeba. They occur in soil and water, and many species live as parasites in other animals. Some cause severe tropical diseases in humans.

pupa The resting stage through which certain insects pass while they change from larvae into adults. *See* LARVA.

R

reproduction The whole process of producing a new individual of a species. There are two types of reproduction: sexual and asexual. Sexual reproduction involves the joining of male and female sex cells. In asexual reproduction, there are no special cells; pieces of the parent break away and grow into new individuals. Some single-celled animals reproduce by simply splitting into two equal new cells. *See* FERTILIZATION; HERMAPHRODITE.

reptiles A group of backboned animals, most of which have dry scaly skins and lay shelled eggs. Snakes, lizards, crocodiles, alligators, tortoises, and turtles are reptiles. Reptiles are cold-blooded.

respiration The series of chemical processes that takes place in an animal to release energy from its food materials. Respiration involves getting oxygen from the surrounding air or water, taking the oxygen to where it is needed, and then combining it with the food materials to release energy and waste products.

ruminants Plant-eating mammals that chew the cud. That is, unchewed food is swallowed, partly digested, brought back into the mouth (regurgitated), and then thoroughly chewed before being passed back into the stomach. Ruminants include antelopes, cattle, deer, giraffes, and sheep. *See* UNGULATES.

S

skeleton The hard, supporting part found in many animals, which also gives protection and provides firm attachment for the muscles. There are two types of skeleton: exoskeleton and endoskeleton. An exoskeleton is on the outside of the body; an endoskeleton is inside. The hard casings of arthropods are exoskeletons.

species A group of animals that share a great many characteristics and can usually breed among themselves. They cannot normally breed with other species to produce fertile offspring. Species is the smallest unit of classification normally used, although it may be divided into subspecies, races, or varieties. *See* BINOMIAL SYSTEM.

sponges One of the most primitive forms of many-celled animals. Most sponges live in the sea. All sponges are attached to shells or rocks.

symbiosis A close association between two animals of different species that helps both of them. For example, the egret, which lives on or close to the rhinoceros, eats insects stirred up by the rhinoceros's hoofs. In return, when the bird is disturbed, the rhinoceros is warned of possible danger.

T

territory An area ruled by an animal or family of animals, especially for the purpose of breeding. Rival male animals stake out their territories by calling, sing-ing, displaying bright colors, leaving a smell, or some show of strength.

thorax In mammals, the thorax is the part of the body that contains the heart and the lungs. In insects and other arthropods, the thorax is the middle part of the body, between the head and the abdomen. *See* INSECTS; MAMMALS.

U

ungulates The mammals with hoofs. They are plant-eating animals. There are three groups of ungulates: even-toed and odd-toed, and another that includes elephants. Deer, sheep, cattle, pigs, giraffes, and hippopotamuses are even-toed. Horses, tapirs, and rhinoceroses are odd-toed. Most even-toed ungulates are ruminants, and have outgrowths on their heads: antelopes and cattle, for example, have horns; deer have antlers.

V

vector An animal that carries a disease-causing organism from one animal to another. For example, the blood-sucking tsetse fly is the vector of the parasite that causes sleeping sickness.

vertebrates The group of animals with backbones. They also have an entire skeleton made of bone or cartilage. Vertebrates include amphibians, birds, fishes, mammals, and reptiles. *See* INVERTEBRATES.

W

Wallace, Alfred Russel (1823–1913) Naturalist who supported Darwin's theory of evolution. Wallace had independently offered a similar theory at about the same time. *See* DARWIN, CHARLES.

warm-blooded Animals that can keep their body temperature constant, regardless of the outside temperature, are said to be warm-blooded. Only mammals and birds are warm-blooded. *See* COLD-BLOODED.

warning coloration The distinctive colors or markings on animals that predators find unpleasant to eat. Some harmless animals gain protection by mimicking the coloration of distasteful animals. *See* MIMICRY.

Y

yolk The store of food in the eggs of most animals.